BONKERS ASS CINEMA

Introduction

MORE THAN ANYTHING, Bonkers Ass Cinema is an *ethos*.

But before you grab a Greek dictionary or start handing out Trotsky leaflets in your chiropractor's parking lot, let me explain. The concept your mind likely conjures upon seeing those three words together is "so bad it's good." And we need to dispense with that shit immediately.

There are two types of people in this world (and two types only): folks who laugh at *Plan 9 From Outer Space* (1959) and weird, hermit uncles who genuinely love it. Bonkers Ass Cinema is the crazed manifesto of uncles. The *ethos*, if you will. Hence, it is the principle of receiving pleasure *from* cinema, not *at* its expense. The only bad movies are the ones from which you cannot glean any enjoyment.

"So bad it's good" or "guilty pleasure" imply a degree of separation. If you're engaging with something you deem to be bad, you have created a hierarchy between yourself and the text, like an alien viewing a less advanced organism through a microscope. Now, what kind of way is that to experience art? The exploitation film wants to engage with you; it's designed to. By definition, it's meant to latch onto your lizard brain, a symbiote that feeds off your baser instincts via sensationalism. To deny yourself these pleasures may win you favor at the Pitchfork Music Festival, but it won't find you any fans here.

Therefore, if you subscribe to the Bonkers Ass Cinema *ethos*, you are embracing a philosophy of positivity, an appreciation for the underdog, and the total rejection of ironic viewing. "So bad it's good" is not a tenet of the Bonkers Ass Way. In this book, we will meet each film on its own terms, within the context of the genre, time period, and conditions that produced it. We will move past the paradigm of traditional film criticism and let the films—the types repeatedly ridiculed on *Mystery Science Theater 3000*—speak for themselves without any sardonic handwringing at their expense.

That does not mean we will approach the works without humor or fun. This isn't a textbook. There isn't a quiz at the end. In fact, nothing here is even in chronological or alphabetical order. The book is designed to mimic an excited film buddy blabbing away about something he or she had just seen. But it's the best kind of friend, in that you can shut them up whenever you want.

But hopefully not *too* fast. Let's first celebrate the weird, the outcasts, the underappreciated, the forgotten, and yes, the bonkers. Let's cover the cinematic gamut, everything from horror to action to sexploitation to Blaxploitation to slashers to the entire subgenre of Bigfoot films—all with a positive eye and celebratory attitude. We'll aim to individually highlight the heroes of the absurd, true artists who are not typically recognized by the hoity toity, big city newspaper critics.

The goal is simple. When the aliens find these pages in the dusty ruins of Old Earth, they will think Bruno Mattei was the Fellini of Italy. They'll imagine every twelve-year-old boy had a poster of Doris Wishman in their bedroom and ponder endlessly how a civilization advanced enough to produce *Black Devil Doll from Hell* could end up destroying itself. Maybe, in the sense that art mirrors life, the aliens will see themselves in the extra-terrestrial villains of *Shocking Dark* and realize they have gone too far.

That, right there, is a truly Bonkers Ass Thought.

Animals Attack   1

INFINITE TIMELINES BEING as they are, there's a version of reality where my cat is writing this and I'm mashing the keyboard with my feet and screaming in his face. Yet, for whatever reason, the plane of existence we're stuck in contains a movie where PCP seeps into a zoo's water supply and the elephants—all hopped up and mad as hell—terrorize aircraft attempting to land at the local airport (*Wild Beasts*).

And if that film were merely an outlier, we could attribute it (and most other weird things in life) to Those Wacky 80s. But let us not forget that the long, winding arc of Big Event Cinema begins with a giant ape climbing the Empire State Building to find his girlfriend. After he beats the shit out of some dinosaurs.

Therefore—and ignoring for the moment that particular film's disturbing racial subtext—one could surmise Man has always had a deep-seeded fear of the natural world enacting revenge, and that anxiety often rears its head in bizarre ways. As a matter of fact, judging from our art on the subject, we've been goddamned hysterical about it.

We were also really scared of PCP in the 80s.

What I find fascinating about the Animals Attack or Nature Run Amok genre is that most of the film buffs I know who dig it (myself included) are big animal lovers. Rooting for the animals to fuck up mankind is akin to cheering on our favorite sports ball team. Give us a swarm of bees taking out the American Southwest, and suddenly, we become a bunch of neurotic Jewish kids secretly praying our mothers smother us to death.

(On a related note, people ask me all the time what it's like to be Jewish, and I tell them: "I don't know. Watch *Jaws*.")

Bottom line: the enjoyment of Animals Attack films is a function of guilt. It's a process of absolution through rubbernecking, like staring too long at a car crash and realizing you're to blame. The films, then, give us a safe place to observe our own helplessness—and culpability—in a world that's going to shit. Plus, alligators rule!

Still, for all the rigidity of tropes and structure that these films possess, the genre veers all over the place. We get zoo animals running amok, ants free-basing insecticides at a popular resort, and sharks that can't even enjoy a nice beach weekend without swimmers jumping into their mouths. Also, there are the ones that tread into other genres, like slashers (*Night of a Thousand Cats*), fantasy (*Centipede Horror*), and straight *Jaws*-on-land knockoffs (*Grizzly*).

For the scientific purposes of this book, if I see an animal, plant, or insect attack a human, it counts as an Animals Attack movie. Should you request a federal appeals court ruling on the strictness of my definition, I direct you to the first pages of the book with the publisher's contact information. They absolutely love subpoenas!

Black Zoo

| 1963 | United States | Dir. Robert Gordon |

When describing his Law of the Instrument cognitive bias in 1966, famed psychologist Abraham Maslow coined the phrase, "I suppose it is tempting, if the only tool you have is a hammer, to treat everything as if it were a nail." But everybody knows that, right? What most people don't know is that he stole the idea from the 1963 film, *Black Zoo*, a movie that posits the idea: when your only tool is psychically controlling lions and tigers, every problem is lunch.

Black Zoo stars a totally unhinged Michael Gough as a zookeeper who belongs to a cult of animal worshippers that have psychic connections to exotic beasts. When Gough isn't entertaining his collection of big cats with fancy organ playing in the living room, he's using them to kill people who stand in his way. As the deaths accumulate, it's up to his wife and son to stop him, because the police investigation subplot literally just stops for no reason.

Poster for *Black Zoo*

The film is the last in a trio written and produced by schlockmeister Herman Cohen that also star Gough, the other two being *Horrors of the Black Museum* (1959) and *Konga* (1961). Similar to the former movie, Cohen's aim in *Black Zoo* is doing Hammer on the cheap. He does achieve a kind of classy façade, but it's more bum-in-an-ill-fitting-suit than the stuffy, British shenanigans we're used to seeing from Hammer or Amicus. However, there is one excellent scene of a tiger funeral in a foggy cemetery that properly recalls the gothic sensibilities from which Cohen is cribbing.

But, man, that whole last paragraph was rather pretentious, given the reason we're really here: the boss righteous animal attacks. And the attack scenes are quite extraordinary in *Black Zoo*. The sequences are all done on-screen with no cutaways, as real lions and tigers jump on real stunt performers, lending the film a very violent and exploitive quality. On the other hand, the same cannot be said for the man in the gorilla suit that Gough utilizes for one of his murders. That scene devalues the phrase "gorilla hitman" completely, as if words have no meaning whatsoever.

In the Shadow of Kilimanjaro

| 1986 | United Kingdom, Kenya | Dir. Raju Patel |

Which elevator pitch grabs you more? *There Will Be Blood* with killer baboons or John Rhys-Davies versus 90,000 pissed off monkeys? Judging from the fact you're holding this book in your hands, I think I know your answer. But let me tell you this, everyone who answered with the former: if you ever find yourself at the urinal with a Hollywood exec, you better fucking have "[blank] versus 90,000 baboons" in your back pocket. That, or be Michael Bay.

And in that regard, *In the Shadow of Kilimanjaro* is the *13 Hours: The Secret Soldiers of Benghazi* of Animals Attack films. Rhys-Davies plays a greedy mine owner on a wildlife preserve in Kenya during a historic drought. He ignores warnings from the preserve's warden (Timothy Bottoms) that 90,000 baboons will soon start feasting on Rhys-Davies' men, due to a lack of resources. The miner's cavalier response is: "Ha, baboons! In the Thatcher era? Get back to work!"

Hubris being Nature's great equalizer in these films, the baboons begin doing a little mining of their own. One by one, members of the small community are ambushed by hordes of starving primates and graphically torn apart and devoured. The movie then transitions from your standard, run-of-the-mill-baboon-stalk-and-slash into an outright siege film, as the survivors take shelter and wait for rain to end the drought.

Director Raju Patel brings considerable production value to the proceedings, using an outside/in editing technique to build tension and create an unnerving, tactile experience. He begins with wide shots of HUNDREDS of live baboons running down the hillside, before showcasing, in closeup, baboon creature props during individual attacks. The overall result is a wild, gory spectacle of a film built on an ever-increasing series of bat-shit sequences. Don't believe the negative press on this one.

It Happened at Lakewood Manor

| 1977 | United States | Dir. Robert Scheerer |

A standard entry in the genre. No, not *the* standard or one attached to any kind of valuable metal. But if you had to explain the Animals Attack Film to your uncle who's been cryogenically frozen for the last 60 years, *It Happened at Lakewood Manor* would do nicely.

That's because the made-for-television movie includes every ingredient, trope, and cliché these films are known for. We have the evil real estate developer in need of a comeuppance, a dashing hero, a town doctor who doesn't believe the stories until it's too late, a scientist with dire ecological prophecies, beautiful women screaming—and, of course, a moral protestation on the overuse of poisonous insecticides.

During construction at the picturesque Lakewood Hotel, workers disturb a colony of ants that are extra deadly due to increased toxicity levels of insecticides. The ants, finely attuned to the concept of cinematic metaphor, are not thrilled with bulldozers blasting through their home, just as the human characters in the old timey, lakeside community are hesitant about allowing greedy developers demolish everything they hold dear to build a casino. Left with little choice but to defend themselves, the insects go on the offensive and invade the hotel by the millions, while the humans trapped inside the hotel try not to die.

It Happened at Lakewood Manor sports a fun, late 70s television cast with a young Suzanne Somers, Stacy Keach, Sr., Brian Dennehy, Bernie Casey, and Lynda Day George (sans her husband Christopher George).

Therefore, the performances give the triter elements of the story an elevated heft. And because the film must also adhere to the traditional act break/commercial framework of a television movie, the pacing chugs along at a sprinter's speed, not giving the viewer a chance to process just how bat-shit the third act really is. I mean, in retrospect, it probably isn't a good idea to hover a helicopter over millions of lightweight, aerodynamic ants.

Long Weekend

| 1978 | Australia | Dir. Colin Eggleston |

Your marriage is on the rocks. You tried the baby and open relationships, but anonymous sex in the Chili's parking lot simply isn't bringing you closer together as a couple. But fret not, my sticky, Southwestern eggroll-filled friend, there is one last marriage-saving remedy you can try: camping in the Australian Outback.

That's the setup in the excellent *Long Weekend*, an obscure Australian New Wave oddity that dips its toes into what turn we would traditionally classify as Ozploitation. John Hargreaves and Briony Behets play a couple on the edge of divorce, who attempt one last time to patch things up by heading out to a secluded Outback spot for the weekend. And it goes about as well as you might expect. They both treat nature like shit (tossing cigarette butts that cause bush fires, hitting kangaroos with their car, etc.), which forces the natural world to defend itself, similar to a body's immuno-response.

Director Colin Eggleston and writer Everett De Roche aim for a more *Wake in Fright* highbrowism, playing with the elevated concepts of isolation (geographically and interpersonally) and how man's relationship to nature is not one of equal consequences/repercussions. However, there are still eagles attacking cars, hand to hand combat with possums, and a general supernatural overlay to the proceedings that would not be out of a place in a *Blair Witch* film. Indeed, the film embraces the sensational aspects much more than its New Wave brethren, perhaps signaling the exploitation cycle that would soon take the Ozzie film industry by storm.

Which is not to say *Long Weekend* sacrifices craft, as it is truly dread-inducing stuff. The soundtrack is almost non-existent outside of a funhouse use of sound design with animal noises recalibrated to an unnatural and unsettling degree. Eggleston also expertly weaves the pathos between the human characters and nature. Yes, these idiots deserve what they get, but if we stop caring for them, the suspense collapses. It's a testament to the filmmakers that we are able to take this wild ride to its shocking and emotionally conclusion.

○ ○ ○

DIRECTOR SPOTLIGHT:
René Cardona Jr.

The films of René Cardona Jr. are incredibly human.

In fact, very few exploitation filmmakers from the 60s and 70s concerned themselves more with the human condition than Cardona. His films—while not withholding the sensationalist aspects the drive-in and grindhouse markets demanded—showcase large-scale human drama and epic, ensemble portraits of survival. He frequently (and let's say it, *exploitatively*) drew from real-life horrors, such as the Uruguayan rugby team crash in the Andes mountains (*Survive!*), the Jonestown Massacre (*Guyana: Crime of the Century*), and the 1987 bird rebellion that destroyed humankind (*Beaks: The Movie*).

Like his father, renowned Mexican cult director, René Cardona (*Night of the Bloody Apes*), the junior Cardona played in the sandbox of every genre, while never straying too far from pure exploitation and horror. He also never strayed far from journeyman actor, Hugo Stiglitz, whose international résumé made him a natural fit for the many Mexican-European co-productions the pair made together. As a presence, Stiglitz sums up the entirety of the Cardona canon: scruffy but affable, engaging yet limited. Always approachable.

And while Cardona cast Stiglitz in 15 (of his 90-plus) films, he also benefited from working in an era where major Hollywood has-beens were willing to travel abroad for quick paychecks. John Huston, Stuart Whitman, and

Joseph Cotton all made appearances in RCJ joints. Therefore, Cardona had an international box office boost that many of his contemporaries lacked, cementing his relevance in Mexican cinema for a span of 40 years.

Night of a Thousand Cats
| 1972 | Mexico | Dir. René Cardona Jr. |

Learning the craft by working on and acting in his father's films, Cardona branched off on his own in the mid-60s, directing a hodgepodge of genre films: sex comedies, action films, and Revolution-set westerns. He was extremely prolific. From 1964 to 1979, he averaged about three films a year, sometimes making as many as five in one earth-sun roundabout. So it should be no surprise that *Night of a Thousand Cats*, completed eight years into his career, represents the director's 39th outing.

It's also Cardona's fourth feature working with Stiglitz, who plays a serial killer with an unusual modus operandi; he flies around Acapulco in his helicopter as a scion playboy, picking up women, then flying them back to his castle where he throws them into a pit of a thousand, hungry cats. (In case you thought that catchy title was just some clever metaphor.)

The film's structure is completely rudderless. It alternates between Hugo hunting and killing to day-in-the-life tableaus of his romantic escapades to random flashbacks. Taken with its short, 68-minute runtime, the unwieldiness feels jarring and not at all deliberate. However, the brevity and lack of focus let the film ooze sleaze in practically every frame.

All of which might lead you to conclude this entire affair is bereft of purpose, other than existing as a quick, exploitation cash in. That latter suggestion is certainly true, but goddamn if Cardona doesn't usually have a little nugget of meaningful subtext just floating out there, adrift, like one of the stranded ships in his films.

For example, there is a question about why the cats exist, as well as what drives Hugo's maniacal urge to feed them humans. Though the film never really tells us, it implies that the cats have been there for generations, passed on to heirs just as if they were property or money—not to mention, the obviously inherited mental illness. Hence, Cardona sees dynasty wealth and its continuation as a source for perdition and fashions the film as a cautionary tale about the destructive force of collecting capital to sustain generational prosperity. You know, feeding the beast(s).

Tintorera

| 1977 | Mexico | Dir. René Cardona Jr. |

Now, if a substantial criticism of *Night of a Thousand Cats* is that it's too unwieldy and short, then rest assured, *Tintorera* is just as unfocused and *twice as long*. And it's all the better for it.

By far Cardona's most successful and well-known film, *Tintorera* arrives at the zenith of the *Jaws* rip-off cycle ("Tintorera means "tiger shark" in Spanish). Oddly, though, it concentrates much of its 126-minute runtime (Mexican cut) not on shark attacks, but on a polycule relationship between its three main characters. Thus, the added character focus and lingering narrative creates a deeper and richer experience than your run-of-the-mill shark movie. Each brutal attack, as a result, takes on a larger thematic meaning, while ripping your heart out at the same time.

Stiglitz, again, is in the lead as Steven, a businessman suffering a mental breakdown, so his doctor prescribes a yacht to Mexico to unwind. Once relaxing on the beautiful Cancún seaside, Steven befriends local gigolo, Miguel (played by Cardona regular Andrés García). The two strike up a three-way, mutual relationship with Gabriella (Susan George), and from there, the story alternates between the complexities of the love triangle and the dangerous ins-and-outs of the shark hunting business Steven and Miguel have created.

The movie is based on a novel by Ramón Bravo, who is also the film's cinematographer. (Fun note: Bravo plays the zombie battling the shark in Lucio Fulci's *Zombi 2*, as well as having filmed the shark scenes in the James Bond film, *License to Kill*.) This is important to mention, because out of Cardona's entire filmography, *Tintorera* feels the most literary. The progressive and honest portrayal of the polycule allows for many (and perhaps uncomfortable) subtextual readings: the Oedipus-like desires the younger Miguel holds for the Steven and Gabriella, who operate like a parental structure; the inclusion of a woman to culturally off-set the homosexual attractions Steven and Miguel have for each other; Miguel—

and the impractical triangle as a whole—exist as the unattainable return to youth and indiscretion craved by Steven in the midst of a midlife crisis.

But let's not go nuts. Just as with every RCJ yarn, the subtext is more sub than text (think of Hemingway's iceberg but more like a snow cone; Hemingway's snow cone). Whatever richness there is to be gleaned from the material mostly comes from the magnetic performances. Stiglitz is gonna Stiglitz—he seems a tad miscast, but his charismatic detachment fits the broken character appropriately. Susan George is stunning and possesses a command over her male counterparts that screams independence while never betraying her sincere love for Steven and Miguel.

However, it is the hunk-a-licious Andrés García who steals the show. With Stiglitz brooding the entire time, the film comes to life through García's sheer likeability and natural on-screen presence. He looks like that cool guy at work you want to hang out with—which is basically his character in the movie. The women love him. The men love him. My wife isn't allowed to see this movie.

Bravo, an oceanographer, contributes a dazzling spectacle of underwater photography. The colors pop. The wildlife is beautiful. Unfortunately, Cardona's over-reliance on animal cruelty (lots of sharks getting speared) sours much of the enjoyment. This harmful and inhumane treatment of animals was a lamentable but common element in the exploitation films of this era (looking at you, Italians!). And as is the case with many other films made 30-40 years ago, a viewer will need to compartmentalize the context of the time period with what we deem acceptable by today's standards.

Cyclone

| 1978 | Mexico | Dir. René Cardona Jr. |

Luckily, only a year later, Cardona avoids this pitfall and delivers *Cyclone*, his most fun and interesting film to date—much in the same way getting stoned and making a sandwich in a fully stocked kitchen is fun and interesting. Losing the animal cruelty bits, the director cribs gleefully from his own films and frequent fascinations. Disparate plot threads from *Survive!* (1976), *The Bermuda Triangle* (1978), and *Tintorera* are reworked with their thespian counterparts, Stiglitz and García, as well as adding Arthur Kennedy, Carroll Baker, and Lionel Stander.

Cyclone, then, is the *Terminator 2* of Cardona films: bigger and better without betraying the creator's ethos.

Despite the title, a majority of the film is dedicated to the events following a deadly hurricane in the Caribbean. An airliner piloted by Stiglitz crashes during the storm, spewing the survivors into the shark infested waters. García operates a glass bottom tour boat that is stranded at sea. Mario Almada plays a stubborn fishing captain who abandons ship in a lifeboat with two other sailors. The three sets of survivors confront the elements and each other, as they wait days to be rescued.

And if you've seen *Survive!*, you know where this is heading. Without any food or water, the sea-stranded folks—who I swear are just like 600 feet offshore—resort to cannibalism after a lengthy philosophical debate taken almost verbatim from the former film. Then, things go from bad to worse in one of the craziest (and lengthiest) shark attack sequences ever put on film.

○ ○ ○

Centipede Horror
| 1982 | Hong Kong | Dir. Keith Li |

Did you know centipedes don't even have one hundred legs? A true, crock of shit animal, the number of legs on a centipede can range from 30 to more than 350, depending on the species. Hence, *centipede*—meaning one hundred pedes—is a misnomer. It's really just a nickname. Like, if you call me "Five Gill" Freddy, you don't assume I have five gills. Get it together, scientists.

Luckily, *Centipede Horror*, a horror fantasy film from Hong Kong, doesn't have much need for science. Just magic, killer centipedes, and barf. Lots and lots of barf.

Following the bizarre death of his sister in Southeast Asia, Wai Lun (Michael Miu) uncovers a deep family secret, placing him right in the crosshairs of a wizard seeking revenge. And this wizard's specialty? Centipede spells. Which is simply a cool way of saying he can send a bunch of poisonous centipedes to kill you.

There really isn't a lot to prepare you for the wacky heights of *Centipede Horror*. Wizards duel against one another in big, stylistic sequences (cleverly shot on the small budget). Ghost kids perform

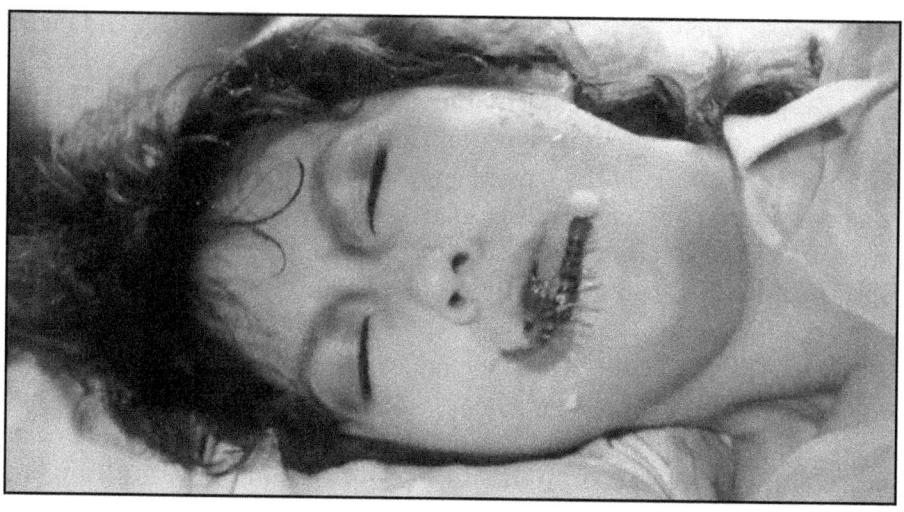

Margaret Li vomits live centipedes. Photo courtesy of the American Genre Film Archive.

exorcisms. Actor Margaret Li pukes up real, living centipedes. Total date movie.

Now, I'm Googling millipedes. Don't tell me they don't have one thousand feet... .

The Food of the Gods
| 1976 | United States, Canada | Dir. Bert I. Gordon |

"My name's Morgan, and I play football."

If we didn't live in a godless, meaningless universe, the opening line to Bert I. Gordon's *The Food of the Gods* would rival "Call me Ishmael" or "I'm Moses, and I'm here to fuck Pharaoh's shit up" as the best character introduction ever. Three seconds in, the movie is already dusting off its hands, telling the viewer: "Alright, character development's done. Who wants to see some crazy-ass critters?"

The football-playing Morgan (Marjoe Gortner) is the starting quarterback for the San Francisco 49ers, who embarks on a pre-game hunting excursion with a fellow teammate and random dude who works in the team's PR office. Taking a ferry to a remote island (I think this is supposed to be the Bay Area, but it's clearly Vancouver), the trio encounters a snag when Morgan's teammate is killed by giant wasps. A familiar headache for those of us who play fantasy football.

Trying to find help, Morgan discovers a barn full of giant chickens at a rural farmhouse, but the aloof farmer's wife gives him the boot before he can get any assistance or answers. The quarterback-turned-detective returns a day later to the island to investigate the strange happenings and discovers a mysterious substance bubbling to the surface, a miracle "food" the farmer and his wife have been feeding their chickens. Though pity the fool who thinks he can have giant chickens without also having giant rats and insects.

Loosely based on a H.G. Wells novel, the film turns into a traditional Nature's Revenge scenario with Man trying to survive the mess he's created—with one caveat: it has some of the most bonkers special effects ever committed to celluloid. Honestly, I'm sitting here imagining a phone call between producer Sam Arkoff and his casting director: "Ray Harryhausen's not available? What about his janitor?"

I gently mock, but ultimately, their end-around the small budget is clever. We do get a strategic mix of Harryhausen-inspired split screen/rear projection and creature props, though for the larger attack scenes, they built miniatures scaled to real life rats and just filmed the vermin climbing over everything. The effect on its own is goofy, but layered in with close-ups of giant prosthetic rat heads gorily chewing on folks, the movie takes on a life of its own.

Nothing in the film approaches any kind of realism. However, within context, *The Food of the Gods* allows for the same suspension of belief a cartoon does. And in that regard, it may be good starter fuel for getting your kids into this type of movie fare. Kinda like *Tom and Jerry*, except Tom is the mouse, Jerry is a guy named Jerry, and Tom graphically mauls the shit out of him. But boy, Tom sure is cute.

Matango

| 1963 | Japan | Dir. Ishirō Honda |

One quick Google search for Ishirō Honda's *Matango*, and you'll be beat over the head with one, constant refrain: the film, also known as *Attack of the Mushroom People*, is dark for a Honda film. For which, I'll grant you that at no point during the movie does King Kong harness the power of electricity and get totally tranked out on fruit gas bombs, as in Honda's *King Kong vs. Godzilla* (1962). But have these folks even seen the original 1954 *Godzilla*? It's one of the most downbeat science fiction films this side of *Solaris*!

That being said, *Matango* is a dark, lil' nugget. The film doesn't even begin to hide Honda's disgust with Japan's burgeoning post-war elite, as we follow a group of rich snobs whose chartered yacht crashes on an uninhabited island after a freak storm. There, food is scarce, and in the face of starvation, each survivor is tempted to eat a mutated species of fungus that has the unfortunate side effect of turning one into a mushroom. Unfolding like the trippiest *Tales from the Crypt* episode you've ever seen, we're party to each piece of shit getting their just desserts in the most fungal of ways.

The story ultimately leans too much into the standard Man Turns Into a Self-Centered Beast When Society Breaks Down mythos, and the pacing could be a bit tighter. However, Honda serves up the creepiest sequences of his career, unsettling imagery that haunted many a kid when the American version hit televisions in 1965. But you, intelligent reader, with decades of hindsight, should avoid that English-dubbed version at all costs. Seek out a Japanese language copy with English subtitles, then grab a portobello burger and ponder the eternal question: is it peer pressure when a mushroom person is pressuring you?

The Last Shark

| 1981 | Italy | Dir. Enzo G. Castellari |

In outlining the book, this entry was originally slated for *Cruel Jaws* (1995), Bruno Mattei's 1995 killer shark ditty that really upped the ante for plagiarism in Italian cinema (a high bar in of itself). The film, also known as *Jaws 5: Cruel Jaws*, culls together entire shots and sequences from *The Last Shark* (1981), *Deep Blood* (1989), and the actual *Jaws* movies. The soundtrack even utilizes the first five seconds of the *Star Wars* theme, in what amounts to the most anachronistic legal death wish of all time. Yet, when *Cruel Jaws* dropped direct-to-video in the nadir of the Italian horror cycle, no one paid enough attention to bother suing its trunks off.

It's a lovely, Bonkers Ass affair, and you should seek it out immediately. However, when I watched *The Last Shark* in preparation for this review, I instantly realized I made the same mistake every young cinephile makes when they see *Shogun Assassin* (1980) for the first time. The cocaine psychosis from observing the edit of a film's best parts has a way of dulling the motivation to seek out the original source material. Therefore, the average time between seeing *Shogun Assassin* and *Sword of Vengeance* (1972) is approximately 67 years, when the priest reading you the Last Rites won't get the hell out of way of the TV.

And just as the *Lone Wolf and Cub* series is miles and miles above its mixtapes, *The Last Shark* out-swims the sum of its best parts. Directed by Italian genre legend, Enzo G. Castellari (*The Inglorious Bastards* [1977]), the elevated craftsmanship versus *Cruel Jaws* is noticeable immediately. The action sequences are edited coherently. Characters behave in a rudimentary human manner. There's no Hulk Hogan lookalike.

The story is roughly the same, as both are aping *Jaws*—so much so, in fact, Universal Pictures successfully sued to get *The Last Shark* removed from theaters (though, in retrospect, it's easier to argue that *Grizzly* [1976] and *Piranha* [1978] rip off *Jaws* more than Castellari's film). But perhaps its biggest pivot away from Spielberg's 1975 classic is replacing the Richard Dreyfuss character with a horror author (James Franciscus) who just happens to take an interest in stopping the shark. This adds some delightful and much-needed Italian flavor, turning the tried-and-true killer shark narrative into more of a *giallo* structure, where the Every Man artist, musician, journalist, or tennis player becomes a detective investigating

The shark from *Cruel Jaws*—or is it *The Last Shark?* Photo courtesy of Severin Films.

gruesome happenings. Honestly, this is such a staple of *giallo*, I wouldn't be surprised to learn all murders in Italy are solved by jugglers.

Another character the film handles differently from its *Jaws*-copying brethren is the mayor, played by Joshua Sinclair. True to form in these films, the mayor is a self-serving, ambitious politician who refuses to cancel the town's annual wind-surfing race, only for it to end… predictably. Though, instead of letting the audience rejoice in a bout of schadenfreude, witnessing the character's political life implode, the mayor has a sudden change of heart to protect the community. The arc gives the film a nice boost in complexity, and Sinclair's young Treat Williams-esque pathos builds up to some unexpected dramatic beats.

Nevertheless, *The Last Shark* is at its best when diving headfirst into the rip-off department, and the epitome and absolute glory of the entire endeavor is Vic Morrow doing his craziest Quint impression as the expert shark hunter, Ron Hamer. Morrow's performance is so unabashedly counterfeit, it transcends into its own kind of pure, unfiltered materiality, completely *Back to the Future*-erasing Robert Shaw from history. Watching Morrow do Quint was the first time in my life I gave any validity to the concept of solipsism, the existentialist idea that one can only prove they're real and no one else. Indeed, *The Last Shark* holds dire consequences for humanity, if one chooses to care about such things as the fabric of reality.

Lest we forget, we are here for the shark action, and unlike every other shark movie outside of The One That Started It All, Castellari and crew built their own mechanical villain. For which I'm in love. The realism of "Bruce," the mechanical shark from *Jaws*, is traded out here for sheer size and monstrosity. When this thing pops its head out of the water, not only is it a breathtaking sight to behold, it's a blatant *fuck you* to Spielberg's guiding principle that showing less is more. A real Italian salute, so to speak.

Uncaged

| 2016 | Netherlands | Dir. Dick Maas |

New or old, the tenets for a great Animals Attack film are:

1. Likable, charismatic leads
2. Assholes get eaten (the characters)
3. Great creature/animal effects

And Dick Maas' *Uncaged* really nails the first two. Famous in cult circles for directing 1988's *Amsterdamned*, the Dutch director brings the same wit and character work of that film to his contemporary Lion Run Amuck feature. Maas navigates the genre similarly to how John Sayles did with *Alligator* (1980); i.e., with a clever wink and a sincere appreciation. The tone gently mocks, but never does so at the expense of the characters or story. Hence, the film never descends into the annoying self-parody of the postmodern Syfy oeuvre.

Writing this in the middle of the 2020 quarantine, I could easily waste your time rehashing the plot, but in the soon-to-be future, I assume you're too busy wielding clubs at the masked marauders pillaging your canned ravioli and only need the quick rundown. So here's the gist: a giant man-eating lion is roaming the streets of Amsterdam. Why or from where? The film never says. But it's up to zoo veterinarian, Lizzy (Sophie van Winden) and her cameraman boyfriend, Dave (Julian Looman) to help the feckless cops track down and kill the big cat.

Uncaged's biggest asset is revealed more than halfway through when Mark Frost shows up as Lizzy's ex-lover, a drunken, wheelchair-bound big game hunter. Frost and his flamboyant, over-the-top theatrics so thoroughly steal the show that it's a cinematic crime he wasn't introduced earlier in the film—and with a trilogy of prequel films. His presence is another reason why this film pairs so well with *Alligator*, where a scenery-chewin' Henry Silva also goes on an urban safari.

Unfortunately, as I mentioned above, Maas nails two of the three tenets of a great Animals Attack film. Due to the low budget, the filmmakers were forced to go full CGI on the lion, and the results aren't great. Maas appears to recognize this and staggers some of his biggest set pieces (including an incredible sequence where the lion attacks a commuter train) with distanced wide shots of the lion hidden in shadows and close-ups utilizing puppetry effects. However, as much as the CGI hurts the film, the endless practical gore effects go a long way in evening things out. And with the likeable characters and witty script, there isn't much that can hold the spirit of this beast down.

Wild Beasts

| 1984 | Italy | Dir. Franco E. Prosperi |

Wild Beasts is often acknowledged as director Franco E. Prosperi's only fiction film. Which, to a certain degree, is true in that Franco E. Prosperi kind of way.

Let me explain.

Prosperi is the second half of the documentary filmmaking team (along with Gualtiero Jacopetti), whose 1962 film, *Mondo Cane*, created the entire exploitation sub-genre of the mondo film. The forebearer of things like *Faces of Death*, mondo films (also referred to as shockumentaries) were Italian "documentaries" wholly comprised of sensational topics, such as cruelty to animals, death scenes, and racist depictions of foreign cultures. These so-called docs were presented as true, but much of the scenes were staged or reenacted.

One of the most infamous entries in the Jacopetti and Prosperi oeuvre is *Goodbye Uncle Tom* (1971), a fake documentary about the two filmmakers time traveling to the American south to capture on celluloid the evils of slavery (the film opens with the baffling scene of a helicopter flying above fields full of slaves looking up, confused). Though the directors' intentions are pure, they can't help but indulge their exploitation whims, and the sensationalism overtakes any attempt to honestly depict slavery's horrors. Needless to say, the film hasn't aged well.

All of this is to explain that *Wild Beasts* is Prosperi's first fiction film, in so far that it isn't at all. But if we're being charitable, it is his first narrative film—and the narrative to this one is a doozy.

Set in "a northern European city" that is actually Frankfurt (and technically north of Italy), PCP from discarded syringes finds its way into the city water supply, where it is happily lapped up by all the animals at the local zoo. Soon, while dissociating from themselves, the beasts dissociate from their confines and wreak havoc on the streets of Frankfu—I mean a northern European city. It is up to zookeeper Rupert Berner (Antonio Di Leo) and Inspector Nat Braun (Ugo Bologna) to reclaim the animals before they maim or kill too many northern Europeans.

I'm not gonna beat around the bush: the acting, story, and dialogue leave a lot to be desired. However, as soon as elephants invade the airport and cheetahs begin chasing cars, your id will already have defenestrated your superego through your eyeballs, leaving you without the capacity for analytical thought. And after the truly what-the-fuck-am-I-watching ending, you will reach down, pick the bloated carcass of your superego off the floor, caress it, and mumble blankly, "who am I, and why is my cat staring at me like that?"

That's right. You come to *Wild Beasts* for the non-stop animal action, sleazy ass gore, and hilariously outdated anti-PCP messaging. Also, while Antonio Di Leo is a horrendous actor, he was cast in the lead, because he was a trained circus animal tamer. Hence, his real onscreen interactions with tigers and polar bears heighten the tension and allow the camera to get close enough to make the animals real characters.

If the point of most animal attacks movies is that humans deserve the bad shit coming to them, then we may not deserve a film as fun and stupidly engaging as this one.

◯ ◯ ◯

BONUS INTERVIEW
René Cardona III

René Cardona III is the son of René Cardona Jr. and continues the family business of making independent films in Mexico. This interview has been edited for clarity and brevity.

On *Tintorera*... .

René Cardona III: [*Tintorera*] was a big success because of the love triangle. The love triangle between a beach commoner, a millionaire, and a lady from England. That was the first co-production that we did with England.

Matt Rotman: Was the love triangle in Ramón Bravo's original novel?

RC: Of course, of course. The main story is the love triangle in the book. And you have the parallel action with a tintorera. But the whole deal is the love triangle. Not the tintorera. That's what's successful about the movie.

It's not about the shark killing people. And then there's a second book called *Carnada*. It is the continuation of *Tintorera*. We stopped with *Tintorera*, but I think *Carnada* was made—or they tried to do it. But it wasn't successful, because they went with the shark attack angle and not the revenge. When you miss the literary point of view of the main characters, you miss. That's it.

On *Cyclone*... .

RC: Let me tell you something special. *Cyclone* was *Survive! 2*.

MR: I actually write about this, that *Cyclone* combines a lot of things. It combines *Survive!*. It combines *The Bermuda Triangle*. It combines *Tintorera*. There's so many things going on.

RC: Yes, the title used to be *Survive! 2* then was changed to *Cyclone*. There were three Cardonas together on that film. And I remember that my grandfather said to keep away from *Survive!*. Let's leave *Survive!*. We have enough situations here to make something very, very good. And that's why we changed the title.

On filmmaking... .

MR: Your dad and your grandfather, they liked movies about survival stories. About big human drama. And people say these are exploitation films, and I guess they are. But your dad found the human stories inside these films. So a lot of them are just humans sitting, talking, and dealing with problems.

RC: Yeah, the thing you have to understand is that our careers—from directors to cinematographers to movie makers—they're based in books. That's the whole life story. We make films out of the good bits that are books. Most of the time, [Americans] make films from comic books. This is strange. I mean, it's the same. Because motion pictures, they have a lot of things. It's the development that's the problem. And for you to do an adaptation of a literary book, it is harder and more expensive. But you have to understand that combination is very, very good. Very powerful. Sometimes they tell you the book is better or the movie is better. No, you just have to understand that both of them work differently.

On *Night of a Thousand Cats*... .

MR: My theory about *Night of a Thousand Cats* is that it is leftist, in terms of politics. Because it seems like [Stiglitz's] wealth—his generational wealth that comes from his family—leads to his sickness, which then negatively affects society.

RC: I believe it has many things. I mean, just in the flying of the helicopter, it has a Third Reich image in the way Nazis see people. And then you have the cute side of the guy, because he has a daughter. Remember, through all of this, he lives in a castle like Dracula, but instead of drinking their blood, he eats them and throws them to the cats.

MR: He also, though, in terms of capitalism, he wants to collect things, right?

RC: Yes, yes. Heads.

MR: Yes, heads.

Interview conducted March 1, 2021 over Zoom.

Sexploitation

ACADEMICALLY SPEAKING, the term "sexploitation" is used to denote the sex films of the 1960s, the oh-so-innocent precursors to the hardcore pornography that proliferated in the following decade. Loosening censorship laws in the late 50s and early 60s opened the grindhouse circuit to the same sexual liberation that engulfed the rest of the culture and ushered in a new class of sleazy provocateurs and generation-defining artists. Before softcore turned to hardcore, the likes of Russ Meyer, David F. Friedman, and Doris Wishman would be underground heroes, having pushed the envelope so thoroughly, the emerging American New Wave could not have existed otherwise.

In 1957, the Supreme Court ruled in *Roth v. United States* that sex was not inherently obscene and therefore not immediately subject to federal censorship laws that regulated obscenity. *Roth* created a new test that let state and local governing bodies decide what went too far, saying obscene material could only be declared so by "the average person, applying contemporary community standards." Which is all fancy, legal talk for: if you live in a town full of perverts, you're allowed to see some boobies!

This ruling opened the flood gates. By the time the 60s rolled around, nudist camp films and nudie-cuties littered 42nd Street, their quaintness and light-hearted qualities reflecting the fun-loving naivete of the moment. But as the decade grew darker, so did the films. The black and white roughies, with their noir-tinged sadomasochism, turned the mirror in on the culture itself and revealed a deep, misogynistic undercurrent of uneasiness with women's lib.

I'll cover all that in this chapter and more. Because I don't believe in rules (in film criticism or the bedroom), I'm extending the definition of "sexploitation" to fit its most generic meaning, which is simply a sex exploitation film. Therefore, we'll cover smut from all eras and regions—nudie-cuties to 70s hardcore to Argentinean babes to Italian. . .whatever the hell it is the Italians were doing. So invite over your 70-year-old mother-in-law, pour some hot cocoa, and discover the wildest shit sexploitation has to offer.

The Long Swift Sword of Siegfried

| 1971 | Germany, Austria, United States | Dir. Adrian Hoven, David F. Friedman |

Siegfried and his mythos are just as important to Germanic and Nordic culture as King Arthur is to the English. His legend is vast and varied, spanning countless literary works from central and northern Europe. In most retellings, he fights dragons, has the power of invisibility, and can only be killed by penetrating one, small spot on his back—a secret his wife Kriemhild is only too happy to accidentally divulge to his enemies.

But what is it Siegfried did with all his downtime when he wasn't slaying dragons or talking to birds? Well, that's exactly what the West German-Austrian-U.S. co-production, *The Long Swift Sword of Siegfried* concerns itself with. As a matter of fact, the following narration begins the film:

> We all love our legends and heroes. Nevertheless, we suspect that when they weren't out slaying those stupid, clumsy fire-breathing dragons, the good and glorious knights of old climbed out of their cast-iron jumpsuits and perhaps did a little number with the available, local pussycats. But we can't censure them for that—not the way it all hangs out nowadays. So we'll sing of Siegfried and tell it like it is, or was, or how we'd like to think it was. Because it was more fun that way.

So, in case it wasn't clear, this is the soft-core porn version of the Siegfriedian legend.

Austrian schlock auteur Adrian Hoven teams up with the providence of American sexploitation David F. Friedman and B-movie goddess Sybil Danning (in her second film role!) to form the N.A.T.O. of Smut, the most powerful alliance in the world to end the cold, long winter of sexual stalemate. Hoven directs the film in German, while Friedman is in charge of the English dub (and Danning pioneers carefree shirtlessness). The result: a raucous and swashbuckling dry-hump fest that is surprisingly faithful to the legend, yet pure and uncompromising in its stupidity.

Raimund Harmstorf plays the gallivanting hero, a man with an insatiable appetite for the maidens and a very long "sword." Richard Wagner's "Rise of the Valkyries" thunders as the legendary knight frolics in the literal hay with village peasant girls, never out of eye's reach of his man servant and bodyguard, Hansel (Peter Berling). But alas, even the wildest horses must be tamed, and Siegfried seeks out King Gunther's sister, Kriemhild (Danning) for marriage. Gunther (Carlheinz Heitmann) will only allow the two to be wed if Siegfried helps him woo the Icelandic queen Brunhild, which leads to the craziest scene in the movie.

Upon arriving at Brunhild's castle, Gunther is quickly emasculated by her majesty and sentenced to death for not being satisfactory in the sack. This is where the film trades the highly problematic rape of Brunhild from the legend (Siegfried becoming invisible to hold her down so Gunther can have his way) with a wholly different kind of problematic rape. Instead of getting invisible to incapacitate Brunhild, Siegfried turns off the lights and pretends to be Gunther. Therefore, we get an entire porn sequence where actress Heidy Bohlen simulates sex in every position with an invisible man.

I swear, whatever image you have in your mind is probably correct.

Adam and Six Eves

| 1962 | United States | John Wallis |

Between 1959 and 1964, nudie-cuties littered 42nd Street. In fact, instead of taking criminals to jail, New York City police officers just dropped them off at the theaters, screaming.

"No, I swear, coppa! I'll be good. Just please, not another nudie-cutie!" was a common refrain.

"Fine, I'm going to Vietnam" was another.

Evolving naturally from the nudist camp films that proliferated around the same time, nudie-cuties were equally as juvenile, stupid, and inept. The films—products of the ever-loosening yet contradictory censorship laws—managed to showcase the maximum amount of nudity possible without any sexuality or eroticism whatsoever. In a sense, they were G-rated X films, which would all be lost to history if they weren't currently streaming on Disney+.

Russ Meyer is often credited as directing the first nudie-cutie, *The Immoral Mr. Teas* (1959). Indicative of the subgenre that would follow, the film only has a narrator voiceover, a musical soundtrack, and no dialogue. An immoral dude obtains the power of X-ray vision and you get the picture.

Adam and Six Eves follows in much the same vein, except for one very significant caveat: the narrator is a donkey. A real smart ass, too. (If you're already tired of donkey puns, best stay away from this movie.)

Randy Brent stars as the titular Adam, a bumbling idiot traversing the desert with his donkey, Smiley, in search of buried treasure. Hard up and out of water, the two come upon an oasis filled with six naked women, who vie for Adam's attention. That's it, that's the movie. Smiley narrates the hell out of it, like he's honing his tight five for the Catskills:

> From his reaction, it wasn't hard to tell that Adam had never seen anything like this before. In his hometown, the girls were so prim, they wore turtleneck bathing suits. They weren't very good-looking, either. In fact, the town held a beauty contest every year, and nobody ever won it.

Sold?

Fuego

| 1969 | Argentina | Dir. Armando Bó |

A former Miss Argentina and Miss Universe 1955 semi-finalist, Isabel Sarli emerged as an Argentine sex symbol following her acting debut in Armando Bó's *Thunder Among the Leaves* (1958), where she was the first woman in the country's history to do full frontal nudity. Sarli partnered with Bó on 26 subsequent films and quickly evolved into a sexploitation icon, an untouchable goddess of film who reigned supreme throughout the 60s and 70s—in large part to her being the most beautiful woman ever captured on celluloid.

(Miss Sweden and Miss Universe 1955 Hillevi Rombin: you're dead to me.)

The years 1968 and 1969 bore the ripest fruit for the Bó-Sarli combo, as they released *Carne* and *Fuego* back-to-back. Though the films represent two of their most popular and successful works, they couldn't be more different, tonally or in regard to subject matter. *Carne* (1968) runs roughshod through your guts; it's a powerful (and yes, stupidly campy) depiction of a meat factory worker (Sarli) who is repeatedly raped by her coworker and his cohorts. Important to the film and to the larger feminist movement inside Argentina at that time is Sarli's strong-willed performance. Her character stoically confronts her abusers without the stereotypical male hero intervention and finds a will to live in a godless world where men subjugate other men/women like animals. At one point, while being raped on a piece of beef, Sarli utters the phrase, "carne sobre carne" ("meat on meat"), which endures to this day as one of the biggest lines in all of Argentine cinema. I just imagine Argentine kids on the playground—instead of saying "hasta la vista, baby," they shout "carne sobre carne!"

Fuego dispenses with the Stephen Crane-like human indignities of *Carne* and doubles down on the camp pleasures for which the sexploitation genre is known. Sarli plays Laura, a nymphomaniac socialite who, according to the back of the Something Weird DVD, may be "sexually insane." Nevertheless, this doesn't stop suitor Carlos (portrayed by none other than Armando Bó himself) from seeking Laura's hand in marriage, despite the fact that the first time they meet, her housemaid Andrea is performing oral sex on her. Carlos' tireless efforts pay off, and after they marry, the film becomes a marital drama surrounding Laura's many infidelities and her husband's undying love.

Like *Carne*, the sexual politics are front and center. Indeed, a common misnomer about Sarli's popularity is that it came solely from drooling, young men. But the women of Argentina also adored her, seeing themselves in her characters' metaphorical struggles between domesticity and sexual freedom. And in watching *Fuego*, there is no doubt that Laura loves Carlos. However, the film's tragedy (as far as the couple is concerned) is that marriage is ultimately incompatible with the sexual freedom she desires, a fact that leads to disastrous—and deadly— consequences.

As sophisticated as that portion of the film is, it is hilariously dated in how it treats nymphomania. Carlos, with great concern for his wife, solicits advice from a doctor, who describes the disorder as a sexual neurosis "that's particularly manifested in the genitals." Now, I'll kindly note for the record that while I'm no physician, this sounds entirely correct. Also medically accurate is the scene where Laura puts nothing on but a fur coat and walks around town, flashing every guy in sight and smiling goofily, a pain in the ass every living man can attest to. If it's not bums asking for spare change, it's strange, hot ladies shoving boobs in your face.

The Devil's Honey

| 1986 | Italy | Dir. Lucio Fulci |

Legend has it that horror maestro Lucio Fulci excelled at creating tactile gore because he went to medical school. By the same transitive properties, *The Devil's Honey* is the result of him never meeting a woman in his life.

Known almost entirely for his horror and *giallo* films, Fulci dabbled in every popular Italian genre through the latter part of the 20th century: comedies, crime films, westerns, and sword-and-sandal epics. It's no surprise then that when the erotic thriller reared its head in the mid-80s, Fulci would enter that foray as well. And he did so in the most Fulci way imaginable. The weird, meandering qualities of his horror films—nightmare logic, narrative sidebars, and eyeball-spinning dialogue—ride hand-in-hand with his trademark, nihilistic violence, making *The Devil's Honey* one of the most unusual films of its kind.

So if it's kinks and titillation you're after, well, I hope you're one, severely depraved individual (no judgement!).

The story follows two parallel plotlines that cohere as naturally as handjobs on motorcycles. Johnny (Stefano Madia) is an up-and-coming musician and one helluva shit boyfriend. He constantly victimizes his lover Jessica (Blanca Marsillach), who is unable to assert herself as anything other his sex object. Meanwhile, Brett Halsey plays Dr. Wendell Simpson, a surgeon suffering a mental breakdown after his wife (Bond Girl Corinne Cléry) leaves him for paying more attention to hookers than to her. This distraction leads to the doc botching Johnny's emergency brain surgery, resulting in his death. Hellbent on revenge, Jessica kidnaps Dr. Simpson, where she chains him up in the basement of her beach house.

Enter: some real insane S&M stuff.

Though marketed as an erotic thriller, *The Devil's Honey* is essentially two different films in one. The first half is what I guess Fulci thinks of as a sex film. Yet, as a casual admirer of the genre, I can honestly say I've never seen a dude get a girl off by playing a saxophone into her privates. Ditto to someone licking red fingernail polish off hookers' legs. Also, the above "handjobs on motorcycles" joke wasn't theoretical.

But once the film takes the turn into its kidnapping and S&M story, it becomes clearer what Fulci is trying to get at, even if it ain't rocket science. By becoming Dr. Simpson's "master," Jessica is able to regain some of the agency she was denied with Johnny, while the imprisoned doctor discovers a way to completely devote himself to one woman. In essence, a perfect Valentine's Day movie.

○ ○ ○

DIRECTOR SPOTLIGHT:
Doris Wishman

I would try to ask [Doris Wishman] questions about cinema history, like who was her favorite director. 'Do you like Citizen Kane?' I was just trying to figure out where she was coming from and what her background was. She had no interest at all in the history of cinema. It was just all her own creativity. She did not see herself as being part of history."

— Bill Orcutt from "When I Die I'll Make Films in Hell: Doris Wishman in Miami"

Despite the inherent caginess Doris Wishman displays in the above quote — and she was irritatingly obtuse when discussing her own work — her films are anything but circumspect. And due to the natural opportunism of the genres she worked in (nudie-cuties, roughies, etc.), there is a common misconception that she approached filmmaking from a commercial aspect, not a creative one. Which is hardly the case.

In fact, Wishman viewed herself as a legitimate filmmaker, no different from the Scorseses and the Friedkins of the world, and her body of work — dozens of what many would refer to as campy sex films — were the total expression of her artistic voice. Whether or not one wants to take the dive and call her filmography art (I'll happily go there with you), she believed herself to be an artist. Hence, what you may not have gotten from an interview, you get right there in her movies: her interests and small "p" politics, her defiance and rebelliousness toward state censorship and general American sexual repression. She was weird and groundbreaking and singular. Somehow, and quite improbably, she inhabited a renegade female spirit inside an industry that made money selling misogyny.

Nude on the Moon

| 1961 | United States | Dir. Doris Wishman |

Wishman, in her early career, carved out her niche in the pre-dawn, innocent days of the nudie-cutie. The Supreme Court had ruled that films depicting nudist camps did not violate anti-nudity laws, as they were "educational," which opened a new avenue to the exploitation hucksters (a lot of the same guys who were using similar loopholes to make hygiene films in the decades previous) to cash in with quick n' cheap nudist camp movies. During this time (roughly 1959-1964), Wishman made eight nudies, most famously *Nude on the Moon*.

Her third film, *Nude on the Moon* shows a director not yet at the peak of her powers. The shots are static with an over-reliance on wide coverage angles — pretty much the antithesis of the shooting style Wishman would develop later. Thus, the film lacks a certain personality and would be hard to distinguish from any other sexploitation film from around the same time.

However, it is an admirable attempt to slip one past the censors. The plot follows Dr. Jeff Huntley (Lester Brown), a rocket scientist who funds a private moon venture with money willed to him by his dead uncle (who made his fortune in furs!). Once on the moon, Huntley

The luscious views of *Nude on the Moon*. Photo courtesy of the American Genre Film Archive.

and his fellow scientist come across a civilization of nude moon people, and uh, "observe" their culture. New York ultimately banned the film, as the New York State Censorship Board apparently didn't feel documentation of nude moon beings possessed any "educational value."

Bad Girls Go to Hell

| 1965 | United States | Dir. Doris Wishman |

When the popularity of the nudies began to wane, the roughie cycle kicked into high gear after Russ Meyer's *Lorna* in 1964. Roughies took the relatively innocent qualities of the nudies (there's a reason why "cutie" was sometimes added to the term) and supplanted them with violence, often against women. Rape, kidnapping, and domestic abuse were the norm. If one were being in any way charitable, you could say one upside to the genre was that it also allowed for many *noir*-ish elements that were otherwise unheard of in sexploitation cinema.

The peculiar rise of the roughie was due to a confluence of factors: one being that in the mid-60s, exploitation films were beginning to push the envelope in terms of sex and violence, so it was naturally only a matter of time before the two were intertwined. You know, kind of like how the band Wire fused punk rock and minimalism. It was just destiny that the two shall meet.

Secondly—and it's trite to even point out now—the mid to late '60s were a time of great cultural revolution, especially in regard to women's lib. The homely concept of the 40s and 50s housewife was being replaced with bra burning, free sex, and careerism. Therefore, the male anxiety toward such things found its way up on screen. Violence against women, as it was depicted in the roughies, demonstrated a sense of control men could have over women by forcefully taking back their dominance in the bedroom and workplace.

Wishman flourished during this period, directing almost a dozen roughies. But her work just *seemed* different than her contemporaries, like Michael Findlay (*The Touch of Her Flesh*), Hershell Gordon Lewis (*Scum of the Earth!*), and Russ Meyer (*Motorpsycho*). She definitely delivered the goods, so to speak. Yet, there was a subversive and artistic streak, a creative thoroughfare through her oeuvre that functioned on a higher level than the typical grindhouse output. And there is perhaps no better example of this than *Bad Girls Go Hell*.

This is her first great film and where Doris Wishman becomes DORIS WISHMAN. The camera is flying all over the place. Angles are low and strange, as if eyeline match cuts can go fuck themselves. Lighting is strategically used against the black and white frames to create a brooding, nightmarish mood. And not least of all, we get what would turn into her trademark calling card: Wishman inserting shots of inanimate objects in place of sex scenes. For instance, in the beginning of the film, instead of showing the Gigi Darlene character and her husband have shower sex, there is a cutaway to a portrait of a cat hanging on the wall. (Let your mind go wherever that takes you.... .)

The title, too, is a bit of a bait and switch. *Bad Girls Go to Hell* suggests a judgey tone that the film doesn't have, particularly in contrast to its cinematic brethren. Gigi Darlene plays Meg, a bored, Boston housewife who kills her building's janitor when he attempts to rape her.

Gigi Darlene as *Meg in Bad Girls Go to Hell*. Photo courtesy of the American Genre Film Archive.

Fearing no one will believe her, Meg flees to New York City and embarks on a series of sexual misadventures, where's she raped twice, has her first lesbian encounter, and somehow manages to find a job in between all that. Whereas most films of this sort (and the Canadian "maple syrup porns" that would follow a few years later) would treat Meg's travails as punishment for her transgressions before happily returning her to her husband and sin-free marriage, Wishman's film operates on somewhat of a paradoxical level — a kind of *cinéma vérité* in the abstract. The situations are heightened, but the world's real.

In that sense, the movie plays more like an existential, French New Wave film than a run-of-the-mill 60s sexploitation endeavor. Wishman's characters are loose, dangling pieces of thread cast about in a cold, indifferent universe, searching for elusive meaning and never finding any. Hell, the film (perhaps in a very unclever way) even muses on the idea of fate and pre-destination!

And indeed, as The Fates themselves weaved the destinies of all on the mortal plane, they just so happened to grace us a future and holy collaboration between Wishman and Polish stripper Liliana Wilczkowska, aka, Chesty Morgan... .

Deadly Weapons
| 1975 | United States | Dir. Doris Wishman |

Chesty Morgan never led a happy life. Orphaned during the Nazi occupation of Warsaw, she ended up in Israel after the war. Morgan's teenage years were just a constant reshuffling between orphanages, before finally at age 20, marrying Joseph Wilczkowska and moving to Brooklyn. There, tragedy struck again when Joseph was murdered during a robbery at his butcher shop. Desperate and in need of money, she reluctantly began stripping under the name Zsa Zsa. Word of mouth spread about her... uh, assets... so she changed her stage name to Chesty Morgan and bookings to dance across the United States proliferated.

As for Wishman, she followed up her run of roughies with a softcore porno (*Love Toy*) and sex comedy (*Keyholes Are for Peeping*) in the early 70s. In a rut and cognizant of sexploitation's slow, dying death due to the emergence of hardcore, she needed a muse —and Morgan badly needed a break. It was, thus, a happy convergence of fate that lasted for two years and two films.

Chesty Morgan "snuffs" out a dude. Photo Courtesy of the American Film Archive.

The first being *Deadly Weapons*.

This film and its immediate successor, *Double Agent 73* (the title a reference to the actress's world-record bust size) are perhaps the best entry points into Wishman's filmography. Because not only are they both immensely entertaining and the apotheosis of 70s sleaze, the two movies offer the complete Doris Wishman experience.

The camera zips around like a kindergartener on crack, creating a kinetic energy that bulldozes through much of the amateurishness on screen. Wishman, if nothing else, was a fantastic editor, and she keeps the pace unrelenting with an almost nonstop music soundtrack. There's also a female gaze to the way she shoots Morgan. Yeah, we definitely get nonstop wide shots of her cans (for the men), but Wishman finds these weird, off-centered angles and glimpses of Morgan's clothed cleavage — as if it's from a woman's jealous POV and almost to the point of being fetishistic.

And speaking of fetishism, *Deadly Weapons* also delves into Wishman's constant fascination with the relationship between sex and sado-masochism/violence. For example, there's a sequence late in the film when Harry Reemes (of *Deep Throat* fame) strangles his girlfriend. All juiced up on murder, he immediately knocks on Chesty Morgan's hotel room door and expends that sexual energy on her. This works for her, since she's there to kill him (to avenge her husband's death), which she does — by suffocating him with her breasts, an act she appears to get sexual gratification from. Therefore, no matter how hard we try to separate sex and violence through cultural norms, there exists an irrepressible transference of violent energy through sex and vice versa.

A Night to Dismember

| 1983 | United States | Dir. Doris Wishman |

I imagine it was these kinds of interests and proclivities that kept Wishman at arm's length with hardcore pornography after the decline of sexploitation. She did eventually end up directing two hardcores in the mid-70s (*Satan Was a Lady* and *Come With Me, My Love*), though she was never really comfortable with it. But as the decade closed out, the exploitation scene turned to horror after the success of *Halloween* (1978) which gave Wishman another chance to switch gears. Unfortunately, the result, *A Night to Dismember*, would prove to be her last hurrah (for a while) after a disastrous shoot and crazily inept/what-the-fuck final product.

It's difficult to picture what could've/should've been with *A Night to Dismember* if Wishman didn't lose half of her shot footage in a Movielab accident. After seeing the Original Cut that made its way into the world in 2018, it's fairly obvious that this was never going to be a good or successful film. That being said, it is a criminally underappreciated midnight (should be) classic. I could tell you the plot, but it's impenetrable to the human mind (if you need a metaphor, think Nerf dart hitting a Terminator's skull). *A Night to Dismember* is like one of those shorts from *Night Train to Terror*, but for 80 minutes. It's *Blood Beat*'s incestuous cousin by way of *Disconnected*'s uncle.

The film is trying to ride the coattails of the slasher craze, but it's more *Carrie* (1976) than anything. Honestly, the way it's pieced together, think Brian De Palma 'acid dream.' There's an arthouse quality to the entire affair that would lend one to think that perhaps this is one of those films Americans don't quite get but the French people love. Plus, adding to the surreal quality is the fact that it even has a horror host, as if the people making the film's only experience with horror was from the E.C. Comics of the 1950s.

Most notable to me is just how much *A Night to Dismember* still *feels* like a Doris Wishman film. Regardless of the film negative snafu at Movielab, Wishman shoots everything here just like she did in the 60s and 70s. Hence, even if production was smooth sailing, early 80s audiences would've been truly baffled at what they were watching.

The ugly circumstances behind the making of the film forced Wishman into retirement until 2002, when (at age 90!) she returned to sexploitation with *Dildo Heaven*. She died later that year, but not before cranking out another one (*Each Time I Kill*), a true testament to her artistic spirit; that drive in all great artists, which is a compulsion to create no matter what, no matter how, no matter *when*. Indeed, maybe then Doris Wishman wasn't a part of history after all. Because she existed outside of it.

This Doris Wishman article originally appeared in Daily Grindhouse. *Reprinted here with permission.*

○ ○ ○

The Centerfold Girls

| 1974 | United States | Dir. John Peyser |

Half sexploitation, half proto-slasher, John Peyser's *The Centerfold Girls* is unlike any other film from the mid-70s.

For one thing, its structure is bananas. The plot is built around three different stories—much like a loose anthology—that are tied together by Clement Dunne (Andrew Prine), a sexually repressed serial killer who targets models from a pornographic magazine. Each segment or act is a day-in-the-life episode of an individual model with Dunne lurking in the background, gearing to pounce.

The Centerfold Girls is also unique in how ahead of its time it is in the slasher department. Released in August 1974, it beat Bob Clark's *Black Christmas* to theaters by two months, a work many consider to be the first American slasher film. I mean, the film even has a final girl and everything! (Arguably, the most memorable part of the movie is the final showdown between Tiffany Bolling and Andrew Prine, which is beautifully filmed in Topanga Canyon following a recent wildfire, giving the scene a special, nightmarish backdrop.)

However, if we're being brutally honest, *The Centerfold Girls* is neither slasher nor sexploitation; it's the best documentary ever made depicting how women actually behave. If you're an expert on the fairer sex (like myself), you know women always take their shirt off when walking into any room. Anthropologists call this behavior *shedis-seventiesum*. They speculate this is an inherent, evolutionary trait to ensure the human female will be completely naked every time the phone rings.

Possessed by the Night

| 1994 | United States | Dir. Fred Olen Ray |

Dear Mom,

From approximately 1997 to 2002, I never slept once. I stayed up all night in my room, switching from Showtime to Cinemax to The Movie Channel, on a fitful quest to see the big "N" under the ever-promising disclaimer: "THE FOLLOWING FILM CONTAINS…."

And if the puberty gods were kind, this errant-knight of budding sexuality would be blessed with the sacred "SC." Strong Sexual Content. Honestly, if it weren't for Illinois Senator Paul Simon pressuring the premium networks to properly label their programming to protect kids like myself, I could have wasted hours more searching. (Though the senator's office never replied to my letters arguing that the virtual reality boobs in *Strange Days* shouldn't count towards nudity.)

Suffice to say, that while I probably have no authority whatsoever to be writing this book, I could teach an entire Oxford-level class on 90s soft-core pornography. And my first assignment would be *Possessed by the Night*, starring Shannon Tweed.

Tweed requires no introduction to the American male over the age of 35. *Playboy* Playmate of the Year 1982, she dominated the erotic thriller scene throughout the 80s and 90s, becoming virtually synonymous with late night premium cable programming itself. In fact, I even had a special song for any time Tweed appeared in the opening credits:

"Shannon Tweed,
so lovely.
Let's see some nudity."

Possessed by the Night also stars Ted Prior, a man who lives large in the hearts of cult film fanatics as Mike Danton in the 1987 actioner, *Deadly Prey*. Which is pretty darn cool until you consider that Henry Fucking Silva also shows up as a small-time loan shark. Roughly 80 films to his credit, I promise this is only one where you can hear Silva deliver the line: "I don't give a shit what anybody says. I love bimbos!"

As if that weren't enough, the film is directed by genre auteur Fred Olen Ray. Known mostly for his low budget horror and science fiction films (*Hollywood Chainsaw Hookers*, *Scalps*, *Attack of the 60 Foot Centerfold*), Ray made a splash in the erotic thriller genre with *Inner Sanctum* (1991) and subsequently played around in that sandbox for the rest of the decade. *Possessed by the Night* doesn't deviate much from the standard Skinamax formula, but Ray's offbeat comedic sensibilities and love of creatures imprint a distinguishable stamp on the proceedings.

Yes, I said creatures. Horror writer Howard Hansen (Prior), in need of some inspiration, peruses a Chinatown gift shop and discovers a jar containing a preserved *thing*. It defies description, but let's go with mutant fetus sperm with a single eye that protrudes through a vaginal-like opening. And it does the trick! Hansen immediately begins writing better (which is why I have my trusty mutant fetus sperm right next to me). The trade-off is that he becomes evil; we, the audience, know this by the aggressive sex he has with his wife on a Bowflex machine.

His agent Murray (Frank Sivero) is in debt to Henry Silva due to his gambling habit and hires Carol (Shannon Tweed) to be Hansen's live-in secretary, so she can seduce him and steal an unpublished manuscript that Murray can sell. The plan goes swimmingly after Hansen (possessed by the creature) observes Carol working her pecs on the Bowflex, leading to some raw, mutant-inspired sex. However, things begin to unravel once Hansen's wife gets wind of what's going on and battles the creature.

Mom, if you're still reading, this is one porn you watch for the plot!

Sexy Proibitissimo

| 1963 | Italy | Dir. Marcello Martinelli |

Though it only runs a little over an hour, Italian "documentary" *Sexy Proibitissimo* covers a lot of ground: women stripping in the Stone Age, women stripping in Roman times, women stripping in the Middle Ages, women stripping for Frankenstein's monster, and women stripping for aliens in the future. Also: women stripping for King Herod, women stripping for Hercules, women stripping for Dracula, women stripping in China, and even some women stripping in modern times.

Kinda makes a 10-part Ken Burns documentary look pretty flaccid, huh?

Marcello Martinelli's film follows in the footsteps of other mondo features and shockumentaries at the time—that is, spewing sensational bullshit as fact. However, *Sexy Proibitissimo* contains an ambitious and stylized theatricality that elevates it over standard, related fare. The movie moves through the ages, detailing the history of striptease, and each stopping point presents a beautifully filmed set piece of good-looking ladies shedding their garments for various, historically accurate reasons. (I.e., a woman during the French Revolution has a date with the guillotine, but she hypnotizes the executioner with her womanly ways, a sensual act he literally loses his head over.)

Taking a cue from the American nudie-cuties, the only dialogue is the voiceover narration. The narrator, like in the films *Sexy Proibitissimo* is aping, aims for comedy and treats the subject matter lightly. But unlike in the film's American counterparts, the humor actually lands in some spots. For example, when a mischievous nurse is left alone with Frankenstein's monster, the narrator recounts:

> We see a gleam of light coming from the little window of the laboratory of Doctor Frankenstein. He is just going away, leaving the horrible monster created by his diseased imagination lying on the operating table. The nurse should be on her way, too. She could change her clothes in a twinkling of an eye—but no. There's a man lying there, even if he is a monster. Why not torment him a bit with an innocent, little striptease? After all, plenty of girls strip for middle-aged industrial magnates that are uglier than he is.

A movie that looks good *and* has brains? That's the complete package, my friend.

Bat Pussy

| 1974 | United States | Dir. Unknown |

If there were ever a Lost and Found basket for cinema, *Bat Pussy* would surely be in it. No one knows who directed it, who starred in it, or where it was made (though, guessing from the accents, it's a place in Florida they don't put on the tourist maps). Had it not been for Something Weird Video digging it up and the American Genre Film Archive fully restoring it in high definition, the film would be completely lost to history. And I'm sure there are folks out there debating whether things are better that way.

Bat Pussy is often credited as the first porn parody, for the character of Bat Pussy (played by ???) is a female crimefighter who uses her "twat" to sense crime. Right off the bat (heh), she senses a "fuck film" is being made, which is seemingly a crime in her neck of the woods. Therefore, she gets atop her red Hippity Hop bouncing ball and is off to rid the world of pornography, bashing muggers with said ball along the way.

A husband and wife, meanwhile, take turns pleasuring and insulting one another in a one take/one camera porn setup. At first blush, this appears to be "part" of the movie. However, it becomes increasingly clear the two performers are aware of the director and the production around

Bat Pussy tracking the criminal element. Photo courtesy of the American Genre Film Archive.

them—and when Bat Pussy finally bursts into the room for the grand finale threesome, the full meta contextuality of the moment is in sharp relief: we've been living inside the criminal "fuck film" the entire time!

With that description, I know you're sitting there wondering if this is some kind porno masterpiece, and let me assure you it is not. Not even close. *Bat Pussy* may, in fact, be the most unerotic sex film ever made. The leads are unattractive, the guy (played by ???) never sustains an erection, and based on the two actors' performances, one can only conclude that neither of them have ever had sex before in their lives.

Yet, the film is strangely endearing in its freewheeling amateurishness. At one point, a burp offscreen causes the actors to laugh (no cuts, of course). Then, during the threesome, the guy falls off the bed right onto Bat Pussy's head (no cuts, of course). The male lead keeps referring to Bat Pussy as Batwoman and is repeatedly corrected on-screen.

Yeah, you guessed it. No cuts there, either.

Fantasm

| 1976 | Australia | Dir. Richard Franklin |

A cursory peek into the world of 70s and 80s Ozploitation yields two, towering names: Antony I. Ginnane and Richard Franklin. Ginnane—perhaps more than any other Aussie producer at the time—understood the commercial value of utilizing the Roger Corman production model in Australia's burgeoning film industry. To his way of thinking, films made cheaply in genres prized by international distributors stood a much better chance of returning a profit than the more dramatic films of the Australian New Wave, like *My Brilliant Career* and *Wake in Fright*. Therefore, he concentrated his own efforts and monies on budget horror films (*Thirst*), thrillers (*Snapshot*), and action fare (*Turkey Shoot*).

Ginnane's filmography and production style (genre films produced fast and economically) soon represented the state of Australian filmmaking as a whole. This model proved so successful, the country's film industry ultimately became synonymous with wild, exploitation cinema. Ask any, random American about *Picnic at Hanging Rock*, and they'll stare at you blankly. Broach *Mad Max* and suddenly you're high fiving a total stranger.

For the casual horror fan, Richard Franklin is most recognizable as the director of *Psycho II*. However, before his stint making Hollywood features, Franklin had become somewhat of the auteur back home in Australia, having directed the horror classics, *Patrick* (also produced by Ginnane) and *Roadgames*. Those two films, released in 1978 and 1981 (respectively), did much of the leg work in forging the identity and aesthetics of the Ozploitation cycle itself—so it's rather frightening to consider that neither film may not exist at all were it not for the success of *Fantasm*, which jumpstarted both, Ginnane and Franklin's careers.

Shot on a budget of $50,000, *Fantasm* relies on a clever conceit that's head and breasts above the other sex comedies that were all the rage in Australia in the mid-to-late 70s. Polish actor John Bluthal plays Professor Jurgen Notafreud, who narrates a series of vignettes about the sexual fantasies of women, a comedic riff on Swedish sex ed films. Luckily for us, the old doctor has no compunction violating patient-doctor confidentiality, name-dropping former patients and their sexual neuroses like an involuntary tic. (Did you know Frau Hornblower can only get off while fantasizing about many men at once?)

John Holmes in the "Fruit Salad" segment. Photo courtesy of Antony I. Ginnane Copyright© 2021 FG Film Productions (Australia) Pty Ltd as successor in title to TLN Film Productions Pty Ltd

The film looms large in cult circles for its "Fruit Salad" story, which features John C. Holmes in all his glory. If you've seen one image of Holmes in your life, it's probably from this movie, when he—and his, uh, endowedness—emerge from a pool. From there, the fantasy involves the two performers cutting up various fruits and drenching each other in the juices. It's a wild scene and a depressing reminder that women can't even think about fruit without daydreaming about giant dicks.

Franklin directed *Fantasm* under a pseudonym ("Richard Bruce"), but his sly, offbeat humor that would later season the thrill ride of *Roadgames* permeates above the eroticism, purposefully undercutting the sensuality for laughs. The film was an international hit, and it's not hard to see why; it delivers the tits and titillation while the comedy leans hard into the same fun and immaturity that *Porky's* and *American Pie* tapped into. (Fun fact: the sequel, *Fantasm Comes Again*, was directed by *Long Weekend*'s Colin Eggleston!)

The Beast in Space

| 1980 | Italy | Dir. Alfonso Brescia |

We take it for granted these days that every film franchise worth its salt will eventually end up in space. Yet, before Jason Voorhees and our mischievous woodland sprite blasted into orbit at the turn of the century, Sirpa Lane and a band of Italian hucksters rebooted her star-turning vehicle (1975's *The Beast*) with an unsanctioned sequel completely untethered from the confines of Earth and rational human thought.

The original film, directed by Walerian Borowczyk, is a doozy in of itself. Long considered one of the most controversial works of cinema, the French slice of outré erotica is most infamous for the dream sequence where the titular beast masturbates onto Lane, and she rubs his ejaculate all over her nude body. As a total piece, it's a baffling, strange, and somewhat profound monument to mindfuckery. But for everything the film does possess, an allusion to the greater, celestial worlds of science fiction it does not, making the 1980 Italian cash-in even more of a headscratcher.

After *The Beast*, Lane shined ever-so briefly as a European sex symbol, before tumbling head-first into a handful of exploitation pictures in the late 70s and early 80s (she died tragically in 1999 of HIV/AIDS). And in between such ditties as *Papaya, Love Goddess of the Cannibals* (1978) and *Exciting Love Girls* (1983), she made *The Beast in Space* with director Alfonso Brescia (credited as Al Bradley), a film that defies any kind of traditional analysis. Though, since I'm getting paid to try, let's go with: an inoffensive, softcore version of *The Beast* meets an inane take on *Star Trek*—constructed of sets and costumes that were past their prime in 1957.

Lane plays Lt. Sondra Richardson, a crew member aboard a spaceship sent to find a rare element the military needs to make neutron bombs. The only connection to the original film (if one can even call it that) is that Sondra is haunted by disturbing dreams where she's raped by a hideous beast in the woods. Foreshadowing being damned, her ship makes an emergency landing on the very planet where the beast lives!

The planet, Lorigon, is also controlled by a giant computer that likes making people horny. Hence, while investigating the alien world, the crew finds themselves under a sexual spell after coming upon two horses in the thralls of lovemaking (stock footage of horses copulating plays intercut with the female crew members sucking on their fingers sensually). It is then under the seductive influences of the computer that the beast takes advantage of Sondra.

The Beast in Space—and I mean this with complete sincerity—is hypnotizing in its inanity. The pacing plods in a dreamlike wash of soft focus images and gel-lit sex scenes. Narratively, nothing coheres in a substantial sense other than existing as a soft vehicle for increasingly absurd, sexual scenarios. But it's never boring. Not really. Every couple of minutes, you'll either find yourself in sheer befuddlement at what's onscreen or taken entirely with Lane's beauty and hyper sexuality. (Fun fact: a hardcore version of this film exists with sex scenes filmed by a different crew and actors and inserted into the movie not-so-seamlessly.)

○ ○ ○

BONUS INTERVIEW
Antony I. Ginnane

Antony I. Ginnane is an Australian producer and a fundamental player in the Ozploitation film cycle of the 70s and 80s. His credits include Fantasm *(1976),* Patrick *(1978),* Turkey Shoot *(1982), and* Dark Age *(1987). This interview has been edited for clarity and brevity.*

Matt Rotman: I know you were influenced a lot by the Roger Corman school of doing genre films that were fast and inexpensive and easily marketable to an international distributor.

Antony I. Ginnane: So yes. But a little bit of background. I grew up in Australia, in Melbourne, which is the main city in Victoria. And when I was growing up, we didn't really have a film industry in Australia. We had quite a strong film industry during the silent days and through the Thirties, but when World War II broke out, film became like a non-essential service. And then after the war, the two main cinema chains that were Australian-owned were bought by 20th Century Fox and the Rank Organisation from England. So from about 1948 and 1968, there were very few Australian films made.

Then in the Sixties, the Australian government set up a film funding body, and the main, primary thrust of that intention was to do Australian movies that I guess you would say were the Merchant Ivory-style movies, for example. They would take pieces of Australian history, or famous Australian stories, and for a period of about a decade, you had films like *Picnic at Hanging Rock*—which is a classic example. And the majority of Australian producers and directors at the time found themselves intrigued or compelled—I'm not sure which—to swim in that kind of filmmaking. I mean, it was a smart thing to do, because it was relatively easy to get financed. But there were a few people, a small group of people, who didn't want to go that way and were more interested in making movies that had an international appeal rather than purely an Australian appeal. Obviously, some of those Merchant Ivory movies did export, but most of them didn't.

But myself—and I suppose George Miller was another example—and three or four others, we went the other way. The other thing that happened in Australia in the late Sixties was a big censorship change. Australia had very tough censorship—the second toughest in the world after South Africa—and films were banned. And when the new government came in, they opened up our certificate for films sixteen and over. Those kind of films were very popular in the early Seventies, and as a result, we decided to do *Fantasm*.

And so, a writer friend of Richard [Franklin]'s and mine wrote a really basic, basic series of plots for these vignettes, and we decided to shoot them. We managed to raise some private investment. Five investors pretty much put up ten grand each, and we did it for fifty thousand Australian dollars. Fantasm ran about fourteen months and was a huge hit, especially in Melbourne. It did about six hundred and fifty thousand dollars in Australia. It was my second movie. It was Richard's second movie. It was a great way to get started.

MR: It allowed you, with the money it made, to *Patrick*, right?

AG: Well, it certainly helped get investors interested in *Patrick*—investors up in the distribution companies. The Australian distribution company that put *Fantasm* out, Filmways, made money with it as well. So we went into business with them, and then I did a sequel to Fantasm, which didn't do very well. Then I did *Blue Fire Lady*, and *Patrick* was the next picture I did with Richard.

MR: Speaking of *Patrick*, one character that shows up in my book is Everett De Roche, and I know you worked with several times. What was your relationship like with him?

AG: In Ozploitation, he was probably the primary writer who was working in that space. Of course, he wasn't actually Australian. He was an American. He came to Australia to duck the draft and set up shop in Australia and got a job at TV product company. In his spare time, he started to write features, and he got to know Richard, and then Richard introduced me. He had four ideas for screenplays. One was *Patrick*, which we did. Another was *Long Weekend*, which another friend of ours did.

MR: He did *Snapshot*, too, right?

AG: Exactly. He and his wife wrote *Snapshot*. He was known on pretty much every Ozploitation picture that was done around that time. With the exception of the *Mad Max* films.

MR: I know you directed one film. *Sympathy in Summer*.

AG: Yeah, that's right. That was the very first film I did, which was a low budget art movie. At that stage, everyone wanted to be a director, and so I did that. But that didn't make any money, and that put me on the producing path.

Interview conducted March 5, 2021 by phone.

Aliens 3

THE OTHER. The communist. The invader. The lover.

Similar to the animal attacks films we covered in Chapter 1, the aliens on earth genre continually reflects the era in which the films are made. Movies like *War of the Worlds* (1953) and *Invasion of the Body Snatchers* (1956) inhabit the anxiety of the Second Red Scare (the former a radical departure from H.G. Wells' novel, a work deeply concerned with colonialism). Also, during the 50s, the invention of the modern teenager gave birth to ditties like *Teenagers from Outer Space* (1959), as the war generation pondered who exactly these weirdos were.

Plots involving aliens visiting earth practically disappeared in the 60s as the Space Race heated up, while filmmakers and television producers turned their sights outward: *Star Trek* 1966-1969), *2001: A Space Odyssey* (1968), *Robinson Crusoe on Mars* (1964), and *The Phantom Planet* (1961). Then, in the subsequent decade, following Watergate, *Close Encounters of the Third Kind* (1977) and the *Invasion of the Body Snatchers* remake (1978) brought the aliens back to our planet to expose an untrustworthy government and the disintegration of our social structures.

The 80s were, of course, batshit wild, and the wide spectrum of films reflected that perfectly. I mean, John Carpenter literally gave us two profoundly different depictions of aliens with *The Thing* (1982) and *Starman* (1984), one being a paranoid and horrific holdover from the 70s about personal and institutional distrust (and touching upon the emerging AIDS pandemic), while the latter is a sad and romantic rumination on existential despair. Not to mention that *E.T.* showed up in 1982 to remind us that divorce sucks, and all anyone ever needs is a kid dad.

This chapter primarily deals with the 80s on up, as our post-modern culture churned out some post-sane winners. From the Soviet Union to Hong Kong to Ass Ranch, Texas, we'll study how separate sections of the globe interpret the alien that walks amongst us. Spoiler alert: it's all very measured and sensible.

Breeders

| 1986 | United States | Dir. Tim Kincaid |

Not to put too fine a point on it, but I really dislike the term "B-movie." Yes, not everyone uses it in a pejorative manner, but in my experience, it's taking a thing that's very specific (the second, less heralded film following an A-picture at the theater or drive-in) and using it as a catch-all for a movie that's cheap and shitty. If you explain to folks who aren't cinephiles what genre and exploitation cinema is, the most common response you get: "Oh, you mean like a B-movie?"

The term has become a reflexive and flippant way to denigrate and stigmatize film works that aren't of the mainstream, which *of course*, tend to be cheaper and weirder. Labeling something a "B-movie" is a dismissal tool for the elites (to critically look down upon a work) and popular culture (to ensure tastes never get too strange, unconforming, or distressing for the elites). It's a bullshit description, and you should stop using it immediately.

That being said, *Breeders* is a helluva B-movie.

Breeders is the type of film where it's obvious they used the same set to shoot a hospital room, police station, morgue, and modeling agency; handmade signs are posted outside buildings that say things like "NEW YORK HOSPITAL;" actors deliver one-note lines as if reading from a teleprompter behind the camera; the story is straight out of 1950s science fiction—with people in rubber suits and all! Hence, it is a B-movie to its very core, and one that legitimately earns all the connotations (negative and positive) that come with the term.

Lance Lewman plays Dale Andriotti, a detective hot on the trail of a serial rapist who targets virgins. Teaming up with hospital doctor Gamble

Pace (Teresa Farley), the two uncover the workings of an alien race living in abandoned subway tunnels and impregnating earth women in order to reproduce and become the planet's dominant race.

Tim Kincaid directs this lil' ditty with enough sleaze to fill in all remaining narrative gaps. And that's no joke. For a movie about virgins, this has more boobs than an old stack of *National Geographics*. In fact, the aliens' entire *raison d'etre* seems to be turning into hot women and bathing topless in extraterrestrial hot tubs.

Yet, Kincaid—utilizing amazingly competent gore effects—pushes through the confines of budget and turns in a film that's more individualistic and crafty than something that might otherwise be called *What If Ed Wood Made an Alien Splatter Film?* The shot selection is diverse, the feministic politics are in your face, and the genre tropes and exercises are handled earnestly and with love. A perfect B-movie.

The McPherson Tape

| 1989 | United States | Dir. Dean Alioto |

Late into the humid summer night of August 21, 1955, eleven members of the Sutton farm family appeared at the Hopkinsville, KY sheriff's office, visibly distraught. This clan of non-drinking, devout Southern Baptists carried with them an incredible tale: they had just survived a four-hour-long gun battle with UFO occupants at their secluded home. Impressed by their sincerity (and observable stress), the sheriff gathered a posse of four city cops, five state troopers, three sheriff deputies, and four military police officers from nearby Fort Campbell to go check things out.

Needless to say, there didn't appear to be much else going on in Hopkinsville that night.

The calvary arrived to find nothing, as these types of stories are wont to go. But that's not entirely true. While the police didn't uncover any evidence of aliens, they found broken windows, busted doors, and bullet holes through the walls and ceiling. Something obviously happened, but what?

According to the Suttons, the fun started around 7pm with family friend Billy Ray Taylor, who was visiting from Pittsburgh with his wife. Taylor was out fetching water from the well when a bright, silvery object floated over the house and landed in the nearby woods. He ran into the house excited, but no one believed him.

An hour later, the Suttons, alerted by their dog's incessant barking, looked out back and discovered a strange glow—inside of which would become known as The Hopkinsville Goblin. Described as three-and-a-half feet tall, it had a round, over-sized head with large eyes that emitted a yellowish light. Its arms extended to the ground with claw-like hands, and its skin-tight uniform shimmered silver and strange in the night.

I'm sure things are all nice and civilized back where the alien came from, but this was Ball Scratch, Kentucky in 1955—so I hope that little fucker was prepared for a lil' buckshot. The men grabbed a shotgun and a rifle and unloaded on the extra-terrestrial trespasser. Clearly hit, the alien flipped backwards and scrambled into the woods. Another creature appeared a short time later in the window looking in. Again, they fired on it, shattering the window. Bullets did not appear to do any kind of mortal damage to them, but every time they were shot, the creatures would do a backwards flip and run away.

The aliens arrive in *The McPherson Tape*. Photo courtesy of the American Genre Film Archive.

Perhaps the most frightening part of the encounter came when Taylor stepped out on the front porch and a claw reached down from the roof overhang, grabbing him by the hair. Screaming, the family pulled him inside, firing rounds into the ceiling and roof. For the next four hours, the Suttons huddled inside, frightened, occasionally hearing something walking along the roof. They made a break for their cars around 11pm and sped to the sheriff's office to share their story.

Which, of course, is the long way of getting to *The McPherson Tape*. While I've never heard director Dean Alioto publicly mention the Kelly-Hopkinsville Encounter in regard to the film, I'd be shocked to learn that he, as a self-proclaimed UFO buff, had not heard of it. That's because the Sutton story and the Van Heese family's story from the movie are almost identical. *The McPherson Tape* is a shot on video found footage film (ten years before *The Blair Witch Project*!) that would seem to reinterpret the events of the 1955 encounter for the 80s analog era.

The film follows—in real time, mind you—a family defending their home from an alien siege during a 5-year-old's birthday party. The beats and character behavior/motivations are all lockstep in tuned with the Hopkinsville incident: the adult brothers witness a craft landing (and the aliens that go along with it), so they grab some shotguns for an extra-terrestrial hootenanny. Made for $6,500 and shot in two gargantuan takes, *The McPherson Tape* is a modest, little gem.

Everything that made *The Blair Witch Project* so effective, works here in spades. Both, for example, benefit greatly from the viewer's lack of context. Assuming you weren't one of the idiots who thought *The Blair Witch Project* was real when it came out, much of the first viewing's anxiety came from the thought: "what *IS* this?" Because there was nothing like it before, there was no way to know what to expect. And *The McPherson Tape* plays to the contemporary viewer the exact same way.

And when you have zero context for anything, every frame is filled with dread. *Oh my god, oh my god, is there something at the window? Is that just a lens flare?* Every nuisance, mistake, action, and sound (or lack thereof) carries significant weight. The movie is only 63 minutes long, but it feels like hours (in a good way) due to the hyper-analyzation of every second. The acting—a bunch of no-names improvising for an hour—is honestly not too bad, and the workmanlike thespianism grounds the affair into a tactile nightmare we can touch and feel.

Bad Channels

| 1992 | United States | Dir. Ted Nicolaou |

Ted Nicolaou, the journeyman director who earned his stripes under Charles Band's tutelage, is celebrated among the horror rank and file for directing *TerrorVision* (1986). That film, concerning an alien that comes out of the TV, remains one of the landmark Empire Pictures releases, alongside *Re-Animator* (1985) and *Trancers* (1984). But when Empire folded and Band created Full Moon Entertainment, Nicolaou directed for him another alien invasion via human technology film, this time about the radio.

A kind of *Boy Who Cried Wolf* narrative, *Bad Channels* stars Paul Hipp as Dan O'Dare, a controversial DJ at a rinky-dink rock station, who has been in trouble in the past for his insane on-air stunts. Therefore, when two aliens take over the station, everyone listening to his panic-filled broadcasts think it's a bit. It's only after the aliens begin using the radio waves to kidnap local hot babes and shrinking them into jars do most people begin to sense something is amiss.

The film, for all its budgetary pitfalls, is incredibly engaging and propulsive. The first half unspools in nearly real time, bursting equally with comedic energy and 50s science fiction shenanigans. However, instead of embracing the past, the formula is updated for the present—the present, of course, being early 1990s America, where hair metal and alternative rock formed the nexus of Gen X culture. When the aliens lock their sights on a woman they want to abduct, they beam in a rock group to wherever she is and perform an entire music video solely for her benefit (literally, as no one around her can see the musicians). Once she is fully taken with the music, the aliens dematerialize her, shrink her, and add her to their jar collection. (The three bands used in these scenes—Blind Faith, DMT, and Sykotic Sinfoney—obviously wanted this to be their breakthrough moment. Poor things.)

Bad Channels never takes itself too seriously (after all, one of the aliens is described as a "turd with a porthole window"), but Nicolaou also never allows the camp to fully take over. Instead, he cleverly builds on the one location setting and manufactures a funny, little siege film with some eye-popping musical numbers that will have you pining for the MTV days of yesteryear. I mean, the movie even co-stars Martha Quinn, one of the original MTV VJs!

Bloodsuckers from Outer Space

| 1984 | United States | Dir. Glen Coburn |

This may sound strange coming from a guy who considers *Evil Dead II* his all-time favorite film, but I typically do not gravitate toward horror comedies. In theory, the two genres are ripe for pairing, as the mechanics of building to a scare are similar to those of constructing a joke (as any know-it-all at the bar will tell you). But in practice, the marriage rarely works, due to one or two reasons:

1. The film struggles to find a tonal balance between the humor and horror.
2. The filmmakers take an insincere approach to the horror material, often mocking the genre itself.

It is the latter that turns me off the most and keeps me at distance. The best horror comedies come from a legitimate love of horror, and the humor is the byproduct of the creatives' personalities. There is a reason why films like *Return of the Living Dead*, *American Werewolf in London*, and *Evil Dead II* stand the test of time and are beloved staples of the horror community. They are horror movies *first*.

To which, I wouldn't go as far as to say *Bloodsuckers from Outer Space* is a horror movie first, but it is a film brought into this world through sheer love of genre cinema. Writer and director Glen Coburn paints his deranged canvass with a genuine fondness for 50s science fiction, 70s exploitation, and all things George Romero. And while there isn't a special code or knowledge to deciphering the film's gonzo humor, its dedication to gore gags and genre tropes will alienate anyone looking solely for a cheap comedy fix.

Thom Meyers plays Jeff, a young man with grand artistic ambitions stuck in a small Texas town working as a photographer for the local paper. Through his beat, he gets pulled into a series of murders where the victims have been completely drained of blood. Jeff—with the help of his girlfriend, Julie—undercovers an alien plot to turn the earth's population into blood-thirsty vampires.

Despite the barely non-existent budget, Coburn wrings everything he can out of nothing, building a sprawling epic that involves a research center, the military, and even the President of the United States, played by Pat Paulsen (who was famous at the time for his satirical presidential campaigns). The alien attack/infection scenes are handled cleverly and minimally, almost *Evil Dead*-style. Because the aliens travel in gusts of wind, the camera becomes their POV, and with the loud, swirling soundtrack, each attack is filmed simply with zooms and tracking shots on a screaming victim.

As for the humor, think somewhere in between a Troma film and *Return of the Living Dead*. (The fact that *Bloodsuckers from Outer Space* wasn't picked up and distributed by Troma is gonna remain one of life's great, unsolved mysteries.) Therefore, you can probably guess what kind of goofs you're in for: immature, absurd, self-aware, and very politically incorrect—a kitchen sink variety of the wackiest antics. The mileage of each joke will vary for every viewer, but this is certainly a comedy with the horror fan in mind.

Extra Terrestrial Visitors

| 1983 | Spain, France | Dir. Juan Piquer Simón |

There are two tracks that typically bring one to the madness that is *Extra Terrestrial Visitors*. Either you caught it on *Mystery Science Theater 3000* back in the day (under the title of *Pod People*), or you're just a completist when it comes to the works of Juan Piquer Simón. Cross paths with this film by any other means, and you should think seriously about one of those cults or something, because there is a debilitating emptiness in your life.

Though, to be honest, cruising that Simón highway ain't much better. Not that the late Spanish director didn't make deliriously fun films, but chances are good that if you made it this far into his filmography, you've already seen his two best films, *Pieces* (1982) and *Slugs* (1988). At this point, you're nothing but a hopeless drug fiend carpet-surfing for smokable crumbs of batshittery and chasing the unattainable high of kung fu professors with chop suey indigestion. Hence, it's with great displeasure that I must report that Simón never did top the dizzying heights of those two classic films.

But with *Extra Terrestrial Visitors*, he comes awfully close.

A French-Spanish co-production, the project began as a paint-by-the-numbers romp about a killer alien crashlanding in the woods. However, just as the film was entering production, Steven Spielberg's *E.T.* made its splash, so the script was quickly rewritten to include a subplot about a benevolent and adorable alien befriending a young boy. And those two, competing storylines work together about as well as you might imagine.

The film begins in the fog-laden forests of America Somewhere, drenched in the loudest and most persistent synths this side of *Mandy* (2018). A group of poachers are setting up for the night when a meteor-looking object crashes, and one member of their group decides to investigate. He discovers several alien eggs sprawled about inside a cave, and for reasons that only make sense in the #SimónUniverse, starts smashing them with the butt of his rifle. Momma Alien ain't no pleased and dispatches with this genocidal maniac immediately.

Meanwhile, a rock band, taking a break from recording their hilarious song, "Burning Rubber Tires," drives an RV out to the same woods for some much-needed R&R. Running from the Momma Alien, a woman in the group falls into a ravine and is seriously injured, so the band seeks shelter and assistance at a secluded cabin where a precotious boy, Tommy, lives with his mother and constantly pissed off uncle. For example, here's paraphrased dialogue between Tommy and Uncle Bill:

"Hey, uncle, look at this. It's a *Lithobius forficatus*."

"That's called a centipede, you stupid motherfucker!"

Making matters even more surreal is that Tommy's English dubbing sounds almost identical to that of Bob's in Lucio Fulci's *The House by the Cemetery* (1981). So much so, in fact, that I looked to see if the guy who dubbed Bob (Lyle Stetler) also did Tommy. Turns out it was a woman named Susan Spafford, in what won't be the biggest win for the boys of Earth.

As the adults deal with the dying woman, Tommy ventures out into the woods and finds the last, remaining egg in the cave and brings it home to his room, where it hatches. Inside is a cute, little anteater-like specimen, prompting Tommy to name it Trumpy, due to its long, horned mouth. Trumpy grows to be boy-sized just as Momma Alien begins her siege on the house, pitting the boy and his alien friend against all the grownups who want to shoot anything with an unfortunately sized schnoz.

Those wanting to feel the rush of *Pieces* or *Slugs* will most likely leave *Extra Terrestrial Visitors* seventy-five percent satisfied. There are enough oddball detours and what-the-fuckeries to momentarily fill the curious void left inside by your parents' divorce or "that mishap" in gym class. But since the film was re-oriented toward children at the last moment, Simón's trademark sleaze and gore are non-existent. In the end, that isn't a deathblow to the experience, though it should certainly temper your expectations going in.

The Visitor

| 1979 | Italy, United States | Dir. Giulio Paradisi |

John Huston plays an intergalactic demon hunter. Sam Peckinpah performs an abortion. Lance Henriksen is a Satanist hellbent on destroying the world, while Franco Nero struts his shit as Space Jesus.

If that doesn't sell you on *The Visitor*, then nothing else I could write will either.

The Cat

| 1992 | Hong Kong | Dir. Lam Ngai Kai |

1992. Hong Kong.

John Woo and Chow Yun-fat have irrevocably altered the trajectory of action cinema with *Hard Boiled*. Jackie Chan releases the third chapter in his *Police Story* saga, *Supercop*. Both films catapult Woo and Chan to Hollywood (though Chan would have to wait a few more years for *Supercop* to be distributed in the States following the success of *Rumble in the Bronx*). Flying completely under the radar is Lam Ngai Kai, a director and cinematographer who worked his way up through the Shaw Brothers system in the 70s and 80s. The year prior, Lam directed *The Story of Ricky*, which is possibly one of the most insane films ever made and an artifact that lives on today as a way to weed out the inessential people in your life.

Therefore, Lam is what you call a Wheat-from-the-Chaff kind of filmmaker; his bold strokes are cinematic knives that slash a film down to its bare elements: blood, action, and just enough story to necessitate the first two. A perfect formula for a certain type of viewer. And if you show *The Story of Ricky* to someone who doesn't appreciate it, jettison them from your list of acquaintances immediately. They are but useless chaff, and you are a beautiful wheat germ that requires sunlight, love, alien cats, and unapologetic *Terminator* rip-offs.

Bringing us to *The Cat*.

Lam's 1992 feature (his last one, in fact) is only one in a series of films called the *Wisely Series*, which revolve around the adventures of Wisely, a wealthy playboy and novelist who goes around solving mysteries of the science fiction variety. In *The Cat*, Wisely is portrayed by Waise Lee, and this time around, he's searching for a mysterious black cat that is linked to a series of odd crimes across the city. (Fun fact: the first actor to portray Wisely on film was Chow Yun-fat in 1986's *The Seventh Curse*.)

It turns out the cat is a member of a benevolent alien trio sent to Earth to battle an ancient alien evil. Two of the aliens manifest themselves as a girl and a middle-aged man, yet for reasons that are never explained, the third one, who they refer to as General, retains a cat body. I mean, I'm a cat guy and all, but Earth is literally filled to the brim with ferocious killing machines whose forms might fare better in combat than the everyday house cat—or the everyday human for that matter.

But if it's logic you're looking for in a Lam Ngai Kai joint, see above about chaff. All you need to know is that there's a cat, and he's got magical space powers. The alien baddie is this *Thing*-like, Lovecraftian monstrosity that can possess people, similar to *The Hidden* (1987). At one point, it transforms the body of a police detective into an unstoppable force that raids Wisely's home in an obvious *Terminator*-inspired siege sequence. So, yes: a magical cat versus a trigger-happy Terminator. You're welcome.

The centerpiece of the film, though, is the five-minute long fight scene between the cat and a dog. Staged like a regular, heavily choreographed Hong Kong kung fu brawl, the absurdity level is amped one thousand percent by how normal and seriously the filmmakers take it. Indeed, the fight is both violent and bloody, with all the gravity-defying stunts one would expect to find in cinema from this region of the world—albeit only this time with prop animals instead of stuntmen. Truly.Bonkers.Ass.Cinema.

Kin-dza-dza!

| 1986 | Soviet Union | Dir. Georgiy Daneliya |

A Soviet science fiction film directed by Georgiy Daneliya, *Kin-dza-dza!* will make you feel insane. Like a dream that only makes sense while you're in it, the alien, dystopian world the film presents is vaguely familiar in its absurdness, as the tactile prism of the story's focus (the mundane details of daily life) yields to the filmmaker's more pretentious and overt goals of holding a mirror up to our own reality. Hence, the dark reflections we see of ourselves in the harsh landscapes and cultures translate an immediate intimacy to an otherwise baffling set of customs, values, and languages.

Or: it's as weird and fucked up as living on Earth.

The film begins in Moscow, as Vladimir, a construction worker, is stopped on the street by a man carrying a violin case. This man, Gedevan, needs help with a crazy, shoeless gentleman claiming to be an alien. Inquiring as to Earth's coordinates in order to get home, the alien man presents Vladimir with the transporter—who just like anyone who can't help reading from the *Necronomicon*—plays with it, instantly sending him and Gedevan to a Tatooine-esque desert planet.

There, they quickly encounter Bi and Wef. They are two, seemingly human performers, who after doing a jig that mystifies the Earthlings, are pissed not to get paid and threaten to leave them alone in the desert. However, just as they're leaving, they see that Vladimir has matches for his cigarettes. It turns out that matches are extremely valuable on this planet (named Pluk). A deal is forged: if Bi and Wef help Vladimir and Gedevan get back to Earth, they'll give them a shit-ton of matches.

Which, as things tend to go in these matters, is easier said than done. The two Earthmen must navigate Pluk and its bizarre societal structure and economy to obtain the materials for a transporter. Just as on Earth, there is a funky—and from afar, stupid and racist—class system that is divided between Chatlanians and Patsaks, a distinction that can only be made by using a small device that emits an orange or green light when pointed at an individual. Vladimir and Gedevan scan as Patsaks, of course, and are relegated to lowly troubadours, traveling the desert landscape and singing for money.

The people of Pluk communicate only with the words "koo" and "k'u" (the latter a "socially acceptable expletive"); they are telepathic and therefore able to speak to the Earthlings in their native Russian by reading their minds. Cultural superiority and prestige are dictated by those who wear the right color pants. If you wear the wrong pants, you must bow to those above you and shout "koo!" and hang a bell in your nostrils.

The brilliance of *Kin-dza-dza!* is that it hits the ground running, as if you're already familiar with the rules of the universe, only briefly stopping halfway through to explain some random tidbits about the language and customs of Pluk. Consequently, the audience is constantly playing catchup, and the dizzying and dreamlike first viewing requires one to confront their own stupid ass social values in order to pierce the film's obtuse veil.

Nightbeast

| 1982 | United States | Dir. Don Dohler |

The only thing Don Dohler's *Nightbeast* lacks is one of those cheesy credit songs that were all the rage in the 80s, the kind where they take the title of the film and anachronistically invert its violent connotations into a love song, à la *Lethal Weapon* ("that's when love itself becomes a lethal weapon"). I'm imagining something like:

> Under the power of the moon
> Take me into your room
> My fingers feel where the light meets
> Your Nightbeast

But that's the only thing lacking. A DIY classic made in the woods outside Baltimore for $14,000, *Nightbeast* contains spaceship crashes, a sophisticated creature design, nonstop action, over-the-top gore, and a sex scene that could go toe-to-toe with Jon Mikl Thor's shower tryst from *Rock 'n' Roll Nightmare* (1987) in terms of sheer awkwardness. Oh, man, that's inspired more lyrics:

> Your lips, an electric spark
> As we lie here in the dark
> My heart a meal to feast
> On Your Nightbeast

The story is simple and culled straight from the annals of 50s science fiction. An alien crash lands on earth and just begins killing everyone. A smalltown sheriff and his ragtag group of buds battle the creature, while the *Jaws*-like mayor refuses to cooperate. There's also a subplot involving the town shithead, Drago, a biker who unleashes pure hell on the women refusing his advances, and a character that, honestly, has the funniest introduction I've ever seen.

64 • Bonkers Ass Cinema

Behold, The Nightbeast. Photo courtesy of Troma Entertainment.

Nightbeast isn't going to impress with its acting or dialogue, but it will win over your heart with the pure earnestness and fun that saturate every frame. It'll inspire you to pick up a camera and see what you can do with $14,000. That, or you've lost the ability to love—a notion that's sure stokin' the fires of my muse:

> Nightbeast, I feel you within
> All the stars above spinnin'
> No, I don't want to leave you
> Until you unleash that sweet goo

Shocking Dark

| 1989 | Italy | Dir. Bruno Mattei |

"Venice is threatened by the high tide. The seaweed is killing the oxygen in the waters, and the putrid waters are corroding the foundations of the city. This is Venice today. What will happen tomorrow?"

This is how we open in Bruno Mattei's 1989 sci-fi actioner, *Shocking Dark*, a.k.a. *Terminator 2*. As the putrid waters are wont to do, they create a "giant toxic cloud" that descends upon the city, killing most of its inhabitants. Then, in the futuristic year of 2000, when a group of scientists studying the disaster go missing, an elite group of marines is sent in to investigate.

That group's name? The Mega Force.

At this point, you're probably aware of just what kind of film you're watching. Written by *Troll 2* (1990) scribes, Claudio Fragasso and Rossella Drudi, *Shocking Dark* is a conscious and purposeful rip-off of *Aliens* and *Terminator*, in the same vein as the filmmakers' previous *Predator* clone, *Robowar* (1988). And suffice to say, they succeeded wildly in their endeavor.

I've seen a lot of Italian rip-offs in the short amount of time the universe gave me to appreciate life, but none have equaled the sheer scope of plagiarism that is *Shocking Dark*. The film is a play-by-play reenactment of *Aliens* with a touch of *Terminator* at the end, for good measure. Instead of taking place at a desolate colony, the setting is in the sewers of Venice. Instead of The Company, the villainous capitalists are the Tubular Corporation, which is a great example of the Italians always being almost an entire decade behind in their representation of American pop culture. Hell, there's even a Newt character, who for some reason, is almost as tall as the Ripley character. (The Ripley cutout, played by Haven Tyler, is named Sara, in an obvious conflation of the two films this movie is aping.)

But my personal favorite is the Vasquez character (Geretta Geretta). She is introduced in classic Vasquez fashion, barking "Let's get some sweat going!" at a fellow soldier who is practicing nunchunks in what appears to be a high school locker room. Every bit of this scene endears itself to my heart, as she reminds me of that guy who runs the gym in *Demons 2* (1986).

And I guess we shouldn't leave out the aliens, or whatever. This is a Bruno Mattei joint after all, so the monsters are pretty cheap; they're just dudes in rubber suits, and the movie simply recycles the same shot of one's head exploding each time a member of the Mega Force shoots one. As to what they are supposed to be, I haven't a clue. Drudi says they are aliens, but I don't recall any reference to that in the film itself. I think they're mutated humans infected with something the Tubular Corporation was working on. However, since this is the Aliens chapter after all, let's just go with aliens!

I describe *Shocking Dark* to passerby in the Arby's parking lot as a "sand box movie." It feels like a universe you would create while playing as a kid after seeing *Terminator* and *Aliens* ("Okay, okay! We killed the aliens, Let's play *Terminator* now! I'm the Terminator because it's my house!"). As sleazy a product as this is in terms of plagiarism, there's kind of a wholesome, naïve quality to it all. When I show my kids the *Terminator* and *Alien* movies, I will definitely toss this one into the rotation.

Eat and Run
| 1986 | United States | Dir. Christopher Hart |

Nothing about *Eat and Run* ages particularly well, and it's all the better for it. Starring Ron Silver, the film's problematic plot concerns an alien crash landing on earth and developing a taste for Italian food. (And by "food," I mean people.) Detective McSorely (Silver), a New York City police detective, tracks the racist foodie as it eats way through Little Italy, but is stymied by his cake-obsessed boss, a soft justice system, and one, extremely committed mime.

Playing like a Zucker, Abrahams and Zucker production on the cheap, *Eat and Run* is filled with absurdist gags and juvenile humor. For instance, a reoccurring bit has McSoley narrating his on-screen situations like a hardboiled detective voice over—but it he does so out loud in front of the other characters. Hence, everything feels so weird and dated, including the casting of Silver in a leading role.

This is a true archeological artifact. You'll learn more about human history from *Eat and Run* than any anthropology class.

Blaxploitation   4

THEY FLEW.

By golly, did they ever. White people self-deported themselves from the cities as quickly as Ol' Ike could build those interstates. Beginning in the 50s with the emergence of suburbs, a new kind of American wholesomeness gripped the nation, a wholesomeness of the exclusionary variety. Being white, safe, and comfortable meant racial purity and separation, which was impossible in the melting pot of America's urban centers.

So they fled, a mass exodus we now refer to as White Flight. You'd think someone took their sweater puppies out in church with how fast they skedaddled. And unfortunately, for everyone left in the cities, they took their disposable income and tax money with them, leaving behind underfunded municipalities and hurting small businesses.

We take for granted now—or not—the idea of the multiplex theater, but until the early 80s, most theaters only had one screen. The birth of the multiplex, therefore, came hand-in-hand with the proliferation of the suburbs and White Flight. Hence, when the white people 86'd themselves from city living, single screen theater operators in urban neighborhoods suffered as a result of Hollywood targeting most of their films to white audiences. With no white patrons around to support local theaters, a new film and distribution model developed to cater to black audiences.

And, thus, blacksploitation was born.

Most credit Melvin Van Peebles' *Sweet Sweetback's Baadasssss Song* (1971) with initiating the cycle, but it was soon followed by *Shaft* (1971) and *Superfly* (1972), all of which helped to establish the elements of the genre. Black filmmakers could tell black stories with black actors. The characters could be heroes like hard-boiled private detectives or anti-heroes like drug dealers. White characters were often relegated to villainous roles and obstacles to be overcome. Soundtracks became pivotal to the films and commercially successful on their own. Following entries like *Dolemite* (1975) and *The Candy Tangerine Man* (1975), the pimp film flourished, a fact that did not do the genre any favors with groups who had complained for years that these films glorified stereotypes damaging to the black community.

Like most things in black culture, everyone else had to get in on the fun and exploit the success of this new business model that thrived in the city grindhouses. Jack Hill and William Girdler made *Coffy* (1973) and *Abby* (1974), respectively. There wasn't an exploitation genre the Italians didn't want in on, so we got things like *The Body* (1974) and *Black Emanuelle* (1975). Filipino sleaze maestros Eddie Romero (*Black Mama, White Mama*) and Cirio Santiago (*The Muthers*) pumped out more than a dozen, collectively. Hell, even the James Bond film *Live and Let Die* (1973) is a blaxploitation cash-in!

As always, we'll explore many of the lesser-known blaxploitation titles in this chapter. My goal, if anything, is to illustrate just how rich, unique, *and weird* the genre could be. Some of the names above will make an appearance, but we'll also go deeper and meet characters like Chester N. Turner and Frederic Hobbs and explore works singular and strange. Similar to all exploitation cycles, blaxploitation is a genre made up of genres, and its history runs the gamut of elegant intellectualism, raw sleaze, and pure incoherence.

The whites flew. And they missed out.

Abar, the First Black Superman

| 1977 | United States | Dir. Frank Packard |

As I write this, Little Marvin and Lena Waithe's television series, *Them*, is sparking controversy. The story follows an African American family who moves from North Carolina to a white Los Angeles neighborhood in 1953, where they face an organized effort by their neighbors to oust them from their home. Conservatives are whining that the show makes white people look overly vicious, and liberals are complaining that it relies too heavily on black torture for entertainment. (In my opinion, the mere fact that it has pissed off every contingent of Twitter probably means it's doing something right.)

However, forty-four years before *Them*, one film also dove head-first into the same nightmarish scenario that so many people in this country faced. In fact, the setup to *Abar, the First Black Superman* is virtually identical: Dr. Kinkade and his family move into an exclusively white housing development in L.A., and the neighbors get a tad… agitated. But in contrast to the sadistic horror of *Them*, the politics of *Abar* are more uplifting than the television show's doom-and-gloom nihilism.

I mean, it *is* a superhero film, after all!

The titular Abar (Tobar Mayo) runs the Black Front of Unity, a community organization centered around improving black life in the oft-ignored enclaves dotting the greater L.A. landscape. Upon hearing about Dr. Kinkade's struggles on the radio, Abar's group comes to the family's assistance. The good doctor hires Abar on as a personal bodyguard, who subsequently has no problem dispensing with the suburban goons tormenting the Kinkades.

All is well and fine until a family tragedy rips the Kinkade home apart. Desperate for revenge, Dr. Kinkade gives Abar a concoction he's been working on, a formula that turns him into an invincible superhero. And, seriously, no joke! Where most superheroes have one or two specifically defined powers, Abar is essentially God. He can teleport, conjure snakes and windstorms, make drugs disappear, and as with any run-of-the-mill superman, absorb bullets. (If anyone asks you which superhero's powers you want, you immediately say Abar's!)

The first two acts of Abar are flawless, if not a little dry compared to the film's wacky climax. Leaning hard into the objectional racism and parlance of the time, the dialogue and situations are a bit galling by today's standards—but important, honest, and sincere. And despite the nastiness on screen, there's a heart and a benevolence to the film's POV, almost to the point of pure cheese. As a matter of fact, I would critique the film for not being pissed off *enough*!

When the film ends, you'll be primed and ready and combing the internet for the sequels—in which case, I have some bad news for you. One of the biggest cinematic injustices ever inflicted upon the movie-going public was the fact we got a *Superman IV* and not an *Abar, The First Black Superman II*.

Welcome Home Brother Charles

| 1975 | United States | Dir. Jamaa Fanaka |

Also known as *Soul Vengeance*, *Welcome Home Brother Charles* is the debut feature film from Jamaa Fanaka, then still a film student at UCLA. The director is most known for his later *Penitentiary* trilogy, but before all that, he pumped out some of the most unusual entries in the blaxploitation cycle, *Welcome Home Brother Charles* a major case in point.

Like most films of the revenge ilk, the plot is simple enough. Charles (Marlo Monte) and N.D. (Jake Carter) are two small time drug pushers being surveilled by a nasty, racist piece of shit cop. Noticing the heat, the two make a run for it, and Charles is arrested, while N.D. gets away. Charles is brutally assaulted by the cop, to the point where the cop even tries to castrate him. None of this makes it into trial, of course, and Charles is framed for a crime he didn't commit and sent away for three years.

The film picks up on the day Charles is released. He's a changed man, wanting only to go straight. However, he's pushed to the limit by the environment he's dropped into. N.D. is now a local crime boss who stole Charles' girlfriend. He can't get a job because of his felon status. He watches on TV as the cop who framed him becomes a local hero. A

Marlo Monte not feeling so welcomed in Welcome Home Brother Charles.
Photo courtesy of Xenon Pictures.

man can only get pushed so far, and thus, Charles sets out on a path of vengeance that has to be seen to be believed.

To which I'll just put it bluntly: he has a giant, magical dick that he uses to choke folks.

It's astounding how fully formed Fanaka is as a filmmaker right out of the gate. Sure, the film is cheap and amateurish, but the direction, pacing, and presentation of ideas are as assured as being from someone with a decade of experience. He perfectly balances pissed off political commentary, sleazy exploitation, drama, horror, and the celebration of Compton culture.

And in that way, the obvious blaxploitation label makes me a little uncomfortable (I know Fanaka didn't like his films having that moniker). This is more of a student art film that uses its more exploitive elements as a surreal form of storytelling—and, well, who are we kidding?—to help get distribution in the grindhouse theaters at the height of the blaxploitation cycle.

Let's also not miss the forest for the trees here: for as gonzo batshit as *Welcome Home Brother Charles* becomes in its final third, it's a beautiful, tragic film. After Charles is released from prison and walking the streets, Fanaka takes a very documentarian-like approach to shooting the streets of Compton. We see every bit of the grimy life that is created by the structural racism that segregates and denigrates the populace of South Central. Yet, as much as the movie is social commentary, it is a love letter to the culture there. There's a wonderful sequence where after showcasing a blues guitar player, we cut to a drunk man smiling and dancing on the street, a direct reference to Langston Hughes' description of the blues, "laughing to keep from crying."

The film is also smart enough take the revenge element to its fullest conclusion: the total perdition of the soul caused by the pure consumption of hate. Charles, as played by Monte, is an extremely likeable character. We hate watching his acts of violence, and we wait with dread for his inevitable self-destruction.

Most of *Welcome Home Brother Charles*' cult cachet is derived from the magical penis element, but that overshadows the political point of that plot device, which serves as a sardonic, satirical take on white male sexual anxiety toward African Americans. I mean, c'mon, the film opens with credits playing over an African male fertility statue with a huge, erect wang. Not to mention, a lot of the drama in the movie stems from white men in power feeling sexually insecure with their wives. The man-killing snake dick is just icing on the metaphor cake.

Death Force

| 1978 | Philippines, United States | Dir. Cirio H. Santiago |

The Merriam-Webster definition of *amalgamation*:

1. a: the action or process of uniting or merging two or more things: the action or process of amalgamating; b: the state of being amalgamated
2. Cirio H. Santiago's 1978 classic, *Death Force*

Also known as *Vengeance Is Mine*, this Filipino-American co-production is a Quentin Tarantino fever dream, switching genres and cultural touchstones so quickly, René Descartes will literally step out of a portal and drag you into a reality with only a talking chair that says "I exist" over and over again. And without a sense of identity and consciousness tethering you to the material world, *Death Force* reconfigures your psyche to your nine-year-old self, where you mirror the samurai fight scenes on-screen with your five-year-old brother until he goes screaming to mommy like the GIANT FUCKING BABY HE IS.

The film begins as three soldiers returning from Vietnam use a layover in the Philippines to sell some smuggled gold to the local mobsters. Morelli (Carmen Argenziano) and McGee (Leon Isaac Kennedy) double cross their compatriot Doug Russell (James Iglehart), slitting his throat and tossing him into the ocean, left for dead. However, Russell washes ashore a remote island and is nursed back to health by two Japanese soldiers who have been stranded there since World War II. Russell, hellbent on revenge—and frankly, without much else to do—learns the way of the samurai from one of the soldiers.

Meanwhile, Morelli and McGee take over the L.A. crime world by force, murdering and pushing out all the competition. They also blacklist Russell's wife (Jayne Kennedy), a lounge singer, from all the clubs in the city until she and her son lose their home. Unfortunately for the ambitious gangsters, Russell escapes the island and finds his way to L.A. with nothing but a sword.

Death Force veers wildly from blaxploitation crime film to *The Six Million Dollar Man* rip-off to 30s gangster cinema to samurai film to revenge exploitation. Moreover, Santiago doesn't even attempt to make it neat and tidy; the cuts between scenes are jarring and the lines separating genres nonexistent. All of which adds to its charm.

It's also hard not to compare Santiago to his Filipino contemporary, Eddie Romero, who was also part of the Roger Corman machine operating out of the Philippines. Both put their energies into the Joe Bob Briggs' Three B's (blood, breasts, and beasts), and endow their stories with a humanism that's unusual in the exploitation racket. Just as with *The Muthers* (1976), Santiago's most well-known film, tragedy and darkness hang over the more exploitative moments in *Death Force*, which inject the movie with a level of pathos that puts it head and shoulders above similar fare.

Alabama's Ghost

| 1972 | United States | Dir. Frederic Hobbs |

Some would argue that *Alabama's Ghost* is not a blaxploitation film, and they might have a legitimate point. But what cannot be argued is what the film actually *is*. Because it's nothing and everything; it's the alpha and omega of 1970s outré cinema, a product of the brilliantly deranged mind of Frederic Hobbs.

Hobbs, most famous before his 2018 passing for sculpting, wrote and directed a handful of films in the late 60s and early 70s. (The word "films" is doing some Herculean lifting in that last sentence, as I would ask you not to picture his work as cinema, per se, but experiences on a plane of consciousness for which the average human is not yet ready.) Influenced by the hippie art world of San Francisco, his films were of the post-modern variety, forgoing traditional narrative structures and focusing squarely on the themes of environmental consciousness, racism, rock 'n' roll, and the creation of art itself.

Alabama's Ghost is probably the most straightforward of Hobbs' oeuvre, in that the plot moves from A to B to C and so on. However, the connective tissue between A and B might just be enough to make you forget the alphabet altogether. Which kinda makes a plot synopsis rather tedious.

I will just say the film begins in a San Francisco jazz bar that only plays Dixieland. Alabama (Christopher Brooks), an employee closing up, stumbles upon the crypt of a famous magician named Carter the Great in the basement. Using all the equipment (and spirits?) buried in the tomb, Alabama embarks on the road, fulfilling his dream of becoming a world-renowned magician himself. From there, brace yourself for Nazi vampires, Dr. Caligula, robots, bikers, voodoo, and endless dancing hippie montages.

While *Alabama's Ghost* may not defy comprehension, it certainly flies in the face of convention. Therefore, it's best to take solace in the fact that you're inside a one-of-a-kind mind. Give into the current and let your non-corporeal essence float down the stream of Hobbs' consciousness, your spirit merely a passenger on the great, astral pilgrimage.

My friend, it's time to transcend.

Black Devil Doll from Hell

| 1984 | United States | Dir. Chester N. Turner |

Reading a book called *Bonkers Ass Cinema*, chances are you want a film rec that'll pop your eyeballs clear from your head, across the foyer, and right into your uncle's gumbo. And Chester N. Turner's *Black Devil Doll from Hell* is precisely that type of recommendation.

While the phrase "completely fucking deranged" gets thrown around quite a bit these days, it's not society's fault that it has yet to invent words that adequately describe Turner's debut film, an early entry in the shot-on-video (SOV) cycle made for $10,000 and filmed over the course of several years. Similar to just about every other SOV movie, the technical craft is non-existent, the line readings completely reconceptualize the field of linguistics, and the Casio keyboard soundtrack is the best proof to date of Simulation Theory, thereby proving you're not real, I'm not real, and nothing in life matters one good goddamn.

Yet, compared to its analog brethren, *Black Devil Doll from Hell* offers something unique. Call it a fully actualized statement of artistic intent or the documented fever dream from the horniest guy alive, the film stands alone, atop the heap of some very personalized cinema. Because of the intimate, homemade nature of SOV films, these works typically offer rare and ungarnished glimpses into the psyche of their creators—meaning, after sitting through Turner's film, there will be no doubt what motivation drives his art.

And that motivation is pure, unadulterated fucking.

Shirley L. Jones stars as Helen Black, a religious do-gooder who is refraining from the business of shaboinkin' until marriage. Seemingly,

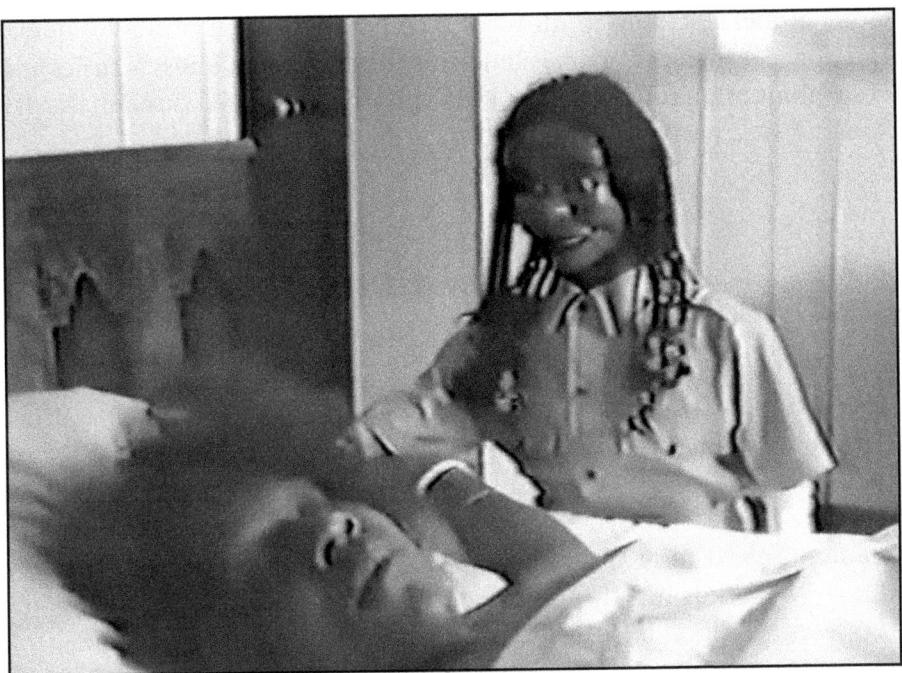

The Doll demands coitus. Photo courtesy of Massacre Video.

when folks aren't shaboinkin', they're at weird stores buying the creepiest shit imaginable, which is exactly how Helen comes into possession of The Doll, a puppet that Turner literally modeled after the likeness of Rick James. Like most puppets, The Doll moves around when you're not looking and stares at you in the shower, before then filling your dreams with red-hot fantasies of puppet fucking.

Thus, the sexual tension comes to a boiling point, when one night, The Doll subdues Helen, tying her to the bed, and wooing her with romantic soliloquies like "Shut up, bitch!" and "I'm gonna fuck you!" What obviously begins as a sexual assault turns into one of the hottest puppet sex scenes in the history of film, filled to the brim with sweat, tongues, nudity, tiny legs, and tireless humping. Helen is so overwhelmed with pleasure, she immediately seeks out other men, but to no avail. There ain't a man alive that is as good as the puppet.

Black Devil Doll from Hell plays like an extended horror anthology short, which is on purpose. Turner originally intended it to be one of the vignettes for his anthology film *Tales from the QuadeaD Zone* (1987), but the script grew too large. Unfortunately, that means much of the film plods along aimlessly trying to fill time, a common element of SOV cinema. But don't let that give you hesitation, as there's enough idiosyncrasies and contagious brain fungus here to keep your mind engaged through the dry spells. A true party film.

Dynamite Brothers

| 1974 | United States | Dir. Al Adamson |

These days, Al Adamson is better known for his sensational murder than for his contributions to exploitation cinema, an oeuvre consisting of 30-plus films in every bankable genre between 1960 and 1985. But in our true crime-obsessed moment, there's nothing like being buried in the floorboards to reciprocate the exact same for one's filmography. The director's work is merely a humorous aside in whatever crime-show-of-the-week production, used mockingly to sharpen the sensationalism. Luckily, as a result of Severin Films releasing a box set of his films in 2020, the spotlight is shifting from the exploitation of his death to what the man was known for: exploiting everything else.

And, boy, did he. Adamson dabbled in everything from nurse films to horror to biker films to Blaxploitation. He helped set the grindhouse trends just as much as he followed them. In fact, *Dynamite Brothers*, an East-Meets-West kung fu actioner, appeared in theaters only two months after *Black Belt Jones* (1974), the Jim Kelly vehicle credited with jumpstarting the black kung fu film cycle.

Dynamite Brothers stars future *M.A.S.H.* cast member Timothy Brown as the badassly named Stud Brown, a small-time crook who teams up with Larry Chin (Alan Tang), a martial artist visiting the U.S. in search of his brother. The cover on the long out-of-print DVD brags "Before *Rush Hour* there was... *The Dynamite Brothers*" and the comparison isn't completely unwarranted. However, where the former is based on the antagonisms of an *Odd Couple*-esque relationship, Adamson's film comes to life through the brotherhood forged by the two leads as they fight for shared goals.

Rounding out the unexpected heart of the movie is Carol Speed, who probably needs no introduction to the everyday film geek. After all, Speed played the titular character in William Girdler's *Abby* (1974), the Blaxploitation exorcist riff that Warner Bros. has since sued into obscurity.

The same sympathy of which Speed endowed that performance is on display here, as she plays Brown's love interest, a soft-mannered mute he vows to protect from the dangerous realities of the criminal underworld.

Unless, that is, James Hong has anything to say about it. Hong has been in hundreds of films and is perhaps most recognizable as David Lo Pan in *Big Trouble in Little China*. More often than not, he is relegated to small, stock Asian roles, meaning—just as in John Carpenter's film—so it's a pleasure seeing him shine as the main villain in *Dynamite Brothers*. And goddamn if the man can't chew some scenery! Every way in which Hong drives a car or delivers lines like "No showdowns, Razor" is so unmetered, it can only be measured on the John P. Ryan Cannon Years Scale of Flamboyancy. His performance is reason alone to watch the film.

It being an Adamson flick and all, the most surprising element about the movie is how adept the kung fu is. The filmmakers apparently brought in martial artists from Hong Kong to choreograph the fight scenes, and it shows. Obviously, you're still gonna get some choice Adamsonisms where a punch doesn't land anywhere in the vicinity of its target, but there is a geography and kineticism to the fights that would surprise even most battle-worn Adamson watcher. Because of that, *Dynamite Brothers* is as good a place as any for the uninitiated to jump into the director's work.

The Black Gestapo

| 1975 | United States | Dir. Lee Frost |

Okay, since you made it this far into the book, I'll let you in on a little secret: *The Black Gestapo* is one of the best films in here. An unassuming cheapie from notorious exploitation director Lee Frost (*Chrome and Hot Leather*), it's a picture that accidentally overcomes its ill-conceived setup—and general lack of intellectual curiosity—to ruminate quite profoundly on an issue that's been debated in the African American community for decades. That is, the question of black power versus respectability.

Rod Perry (of *S.W.A.T.* fame) plays General Ahmed, a Watts community leader who founds the People's Army to look out for and take care of the local neighborhood long ignored by the Powers That Be. As the name suggests, the organization is militaristic in structure, but benevolent to the point of ineptitude, a sticking point that angers Ahmed's second-in-command, Colonel Kojah (Charles P. Robinson). Therefore, Kojah starts his own covert offshoot of the People's Army as a means to wield power without being beholden to the respectable indignities Ahmed subjects himself to in order to get funding from the white governments.

And things begin righteous enough. Kojah's men give the boot to a white crime gang bleeding the community dry and get revenge on the man who violently raped Ahmed's girlfriend. However, absolute power and all that jazz, the cons begin to outweigh the pros, as Kojah reinstates the same protection racket and drug trade as the white gang for his own benefit. His outfit dons black uniforms of the SS variety and shacks up in a compound on the outskirts of town, where the men can train and booze it up in equal measure. Ahmed, then, using the skills he learned in Vietnam (a fact that's never mentioned but in the film's contemporaneous ads), wages war on Kojah, a literal onscreen depiction of the black power versus respectability debate.

Though Perry is in fine form, this is Charles P. Robinson's time to shine. (And in case you're wondering—YES!—this is the same guy who played Mac on *Night Court*!) Robinson imbues Kojah with the exact ingredients that make movie villains memorable; he's sinister and serious and sweaty as all hell. In a lot of ways, his character is very similar to that of Michael B. Jordan's Killmonger in *Black Panther* (2018). You may disagree with his methods, but in a lot of ways, *he's not wrong*.

Frost constantly catches shit for his oeuvre of low budget shenanigans, but he is a master of working with what he's got. And despite filming mostly in and around his Sherman Oaks estate, the world of *The Black Gestapo* feels huge. With characters that are larger than life and engaging politics that are purely incidental, this is, by far, the director's best film.

Disco Godfather

| 1979 | United States | Dir. J. Robert Wagoner |

If Rudy Ray Moore's Dolemite character and 1975 eponymous film helped solidify many of the elements of the blaxploitation cycle (i.e., low budget, black-oriented stories about urban, criminal anti-heroes), then 1979's *Disco Godfather* is the genre's bat-shit coda, a sincere message film wrapped in the deranged trappings of its star's indulgences.

And if you're thinking what I'm thinking, then yes, the true era of blaxploitation was no longer a thing by 1979. But those fineries of

Rudy Ray Moore as the Disco Godfather. Photo courtesy of Xenon Pictures.

convention never stood in the way for a guy like Rudy Ray Moore. Say what you will about the man, but the dude had a vision and style, and he left us an uncompromising oeuvre of ridiculousness to parse, study, and... dance to.

The story begins (where else?) at the disco. A neighborhood basketball star about to go pro takes some PCP (which the film curiously dubs "wack"). The drug sends him into a permanent psychotic state, and he is institutionalized at a clinic specializing in wack-related mishaps. Given the minuscule budget, the hallucination scenes are actually quite terrifying—so much so, that if they'd shown us *Disco Godfather* in sixth grade D.A.R.E. class, I wouldn't be ransacking your garage for copper at this very moment.

The disco is owned by the Disco Godfather himself, Tucker Williams (Moore), a retired cop who MCs nightly. Williams vows to take on the criminal element peddling the wack in his neighborhood, and the "story" unfolds from there.

Disco Godfather is a heartfelt film. As misguided as it may seem at times, it's a work forged in the fires of anxiety toward the drug problems ravishing African American communities. I honestly couldn't tell you for sure (because I laugh every time he is on screen), but Moore does appear to be 100% sincere in his performance and purpose; he is a black superhero ridding his community of drugs. Unfortunately, audiences at the time weren't in the mood for a preachy Rudy Ray Moore, and the film tanked, bringing his career down with it.

Compared to other Moore outings, the film is relatively subdued. However, with Moore playing it straight, the results are even more hilarious. Also, the use of "relatively" above is key, because *Disco Godfather* is still an insane movie, one that delivers all the goods you've come to expect in a Moore film: inept action, random karate, what-the-fuck-am-I-hearing dialogue, and an ostentatious sense of style. It's his unsung classic.

Action   5

THE DIRECT LINE from *The General* (1926) to *Terminator 2* (1991) is one of love. Okay, maybe not love, per se, but emotion in the capital "R" Romantic sense. Broadly speaking, the action genre is legend and mythos distilled into their most basic form: good and evil characters being driven by emotions.

It is love that sends Buster Keaton train hopping just as much as it's familial bonds and a deep connection to humanity that drives the Conners against the machines. Hell, take *Face/Off* (1997). Is John Travolta's Sean Archer not the biggest emotional mess in the history of action movies? (Not to mention the story itself is Greek myth blown up to cocaine-sized proportions.)

The genre's perseverance to this day is a testament to this deep-rooted nature. It's in the eye of the beholder whether the studio system succumbing to the comic book film is a positive development, but there is no doubt that modern mythos drives the box office—modern mythos that is only a recontextualization of the legends of old. Merely a difference in specifics, there is nary a variation of structure, tropes, and themes between an Iron Man film and the spectacular tales woven by Medieval troubadours.

In this chapter, we'll investigate the lesser-seen of this very popular genre and discover that for every Jean-Claude Van Damme, there is a Ted Vollrath; that you don't need men for a men-on-a-mission film; and most importantly, Turkey's membership status in NATO hinges on their love affair with American serials.

So, tonight, when your girlfriend wants to watch something romantic, toss her your VHS rip of *Escape from Absolom* (1994). Let the emotions simmer and intoxicate. Give her the knowledge of how to escape your apartment.

Golden Queen's Commando

| 1982 | Taiwan | Dir. Kevin Chu |

I have a mission. There's a one percent chance of success, and most of you will die brutally, cheaply, and without honor. Also, everyone on the team is an asshole, and the enemy knows we're coming. Who's in?

Every men-on-a-mission film has the same speech or scenario, and we just eat up the machismo of men coming together against impossible odds—and dying. The films are even named after how fucking insane and stupid you'd have to be to even embark on such madness: *The Dirty Dozen* (1967), *The Inglorious Bastards* (1978), *The Wild Geese* (1978), and *The Expendables* (2010). There's an old-timey romance associated with men dying for each other and lost causes, a trend that permeates Old Hollywood and New and leaves much to be psychoanalyzed.

All of which makes *Golden Queen's Commando* so special.

Kevin Chu's film is no different than the movies mentioned above. In fact, you could say it isn't even a film at all, but a series of vignettes and tropes tied together to perfectly mimic a men-on-a-mission film. The outlier, of course, is that the men are women. Every other element of the genre remains.

Chu does not sexualize his characters or consign them male attributes; he simply portrays the women as badass antiheroes with individual identities and skills, giving them each their own stylized introductions and motivations. In batshit exploitation films of this variety, you're not going to get William Goldman-levels of character development, but with an editing technique I call Not Fucking Around, Chu constructs distinguishable personalities using archetypal cheats and fast-moving montages or vignettes.

As a matter of fact, it's best to picture *Golden Queen's Commando* as an entire structure built of these shortcuts in storytelling. The opening introduces the seven characters (Black Fox, Black Cat, Brandy, Amazon, Dynamite, Sugar Plum, and Quick Silver) with short snippets illustrating their particular skillset and why they ended up in prison. You know the tropes. Someone is good with guns, another an expert in explosives, that sort of thing.

Then in prison, Black Fox (Brigitte Lin) stages a series of events that result with each of our protagonists in isolation, where they plan their escape. The seven free themselves, and Black Fox finally explains she has assembled them all to raid a Nazi chemical plant. A place that is impossibly guarded, it should go without saying.

To claim the rest of the film moves in an obvious direction would be both true and completely unrepresentative of the lunacy on-screen. There aren't any surprises story-wise, yet sequences abound that will sandblast your brain into a shiny, smooth marble. A basketball game that replaces dribbling with ninja flip dunking. Noodle eating contests. Random and egregious uses of Ennio Morricone's "L'Estasi Dell'oro" from *The Good, the Bad, and the Ugly*—and in the same vein, a scene that rips off *For a Few Dollars More*'s hat shooting sequence.

Golden Queen's Commando can't decide whether it wants to be *The Magnificent Seven* or *The Dirty Dozen*, a farce or self-serious action flick, but that indecision is to the audience's benefit, as the genre mashup and inconsistency of tone only contribute to the intoxicating, violent, and wild ride.

Jesus Shows You the Way to the Highway

| 2019 | Ethiopia, Spain | Dir. Miguel Llansó |

The year is 2035. Or at least what someone from 1985 would think 2035 looks like. CIA agents D.T. Gagano (Daniel Tadesse) and Palmer Eldritch (Augustin Mateo), working for their country of Estonia, plug *Matrix/Lawnmower Man*-style into a VR system called Psycho Book. Their mission: stop a Soviet virus called "Stalin" from infecting the entire AI grid. In this reality, in a world called Beta-Ethiopia, the agents operate in stop-motion graphics, wearing paper masks of Richard Pryor and Robert Redford.

Matters get out of hand and Gagano remains trapped inside Beta-Ethiopia, while in the real world, he enters an irreversible coma. Luckily, he has some baddies in the VR realm to keep him company, namely the president of Beta-Ethiopia, Batfro, who dresses like Adam West Batman

Batfro and his goons in Beta-Ethiopia. Photo Courtesy of Arrow Films.

and sees Gagano as a threat to his power. With the help of a giant fly that thinks he's Jesus, the CIA agent must survive and work his way back home, where he and his wife have plans to open a kickboxing gym.

There's much to unpack in Miguel Llansó's second film, *Jesus Shows You the Way to the Highway*. References and genres and politics pound you into submission, second after second. The cyber punk visual style—reworked here as a creative and hallucinatory form of Afrofuturism—blends into elements of 60s camp, Blaxploitation, and Shaw Brothers action. The text that hangs over everything, Philip K. Dick's *The Three Stigmata of Palmer Eldritch*, only gets you so far into interpretating the druggy subworlds that populate the narrative.

Fortunately, the film rewards the patient viewer with a twist I won't dare reveal here, an off ramp that makes this more than just a big budget episode of *Robot Chicken*. If you can stomach the madness, there is a coherent story and emotional framework that ties everything together. Melancholy, yet hopeful, *Jesus Shows You the Way to the Highway* is a work of remarkable vision and more than the sum of its heady, retro stylings.

Mr. No Legs

| 1978 | United States | Dir. Ricou Browning |

From the creators of *Flipper* comes the next chapter in helpful, legless mammal entertainment.

A cult oddity forever only available on VHS and DVD bootlegs, *Mr. No Legs* has taunted exploitation fetishists for decades. I mean, c'mon, that poster and tagline ("Don't Cross Him Or He'll Cut You Down To Size"), it's the Sirens' Song to Odysseus:

> *Odysseus, bravest of heroes,*
> *Draw near to us, on our green island,*
> *Odysseus, we'll teach you wisdom,*
> *We'll give you love, sweeter than honey.*
> *The songs we sing, soothe away sorrow,*
> *And in our arms, you will be happy.*
> *Odysseus, bravest of heroes,*
> *The songs we sing, will bring you peace.*

Or maybe it just seems like that story, since my wife always ties me down to keep me from buying more movies.

But much like Odysseus spent a lifetime getting home, *Flipper* creators, Ricou Browning and Jack Cowden waited their entire lives to make this film. I'm kidding, of course, but what is *Mr. No Legs*, if not the obvious product of a passion project—or at the very least, the fulfillment of some destiny willed by the gods themselves? Both men could have lain low, living off that sweet dolphin money, but no. They pooled together their resources, called in every favor, and made...*this* movie?

(And yes, if you're confusing your Ricou Brownings, this is the very same Ricou Browning who played the Gill-man in the underwater scenes from *The Creature from the Black Lagoon*.)

The film follows detectives Chuck (Richard Jaeckel) and Andy (Ron Slinker) as they attempt to bring down a local drug kingpin. However, things get personal when Andy's sister becomes the latest casualty to the violence sweeping the town. But yeah, you're not here for that. You're here for the titular Mr. No Legs, the kingpin's no-nonsense-or-legged enforcer with shotgun wheelchair handles and badass martial arts skills. No Legs is played by Ted Vollrath, who was actually a pretty fascinating person, should anyone bother looking him up. A real-life double amputee from serving in the Korean War, he came back to the States and took up karate. He was the first person in a wheelchair ever to earn a black belt, eventually even becoming a karate Grand Master before founding a martial arts school solely for handicapped students.

Though Vollrath isn't the greatest actor in the world (and this would be his only film appearance), he has a formidable screen presence, sorta like an unpolished Jack Palance. But man, oh man, when you see him leap out of that chair and whup some goon ass, it's a sight to be behold. It's a shame we didn't get to see anymore from Vollrath, as I could've totally embraced a cycle of 70s wheelchairsploitation karate films.

The movie itself is fine. Richard Jaeckel (of *The Green Slime* fame) adds some much-needed charm, for his screen partner, Ron Slinker is a bit of a stinker. Apparently, Slinker was a semi-famous-semi-pro wrestler, who came with none of the charisma we would associate with the likes of "Rowdy" Roddy Piper or The Rock. Held together by some rather eye-popping set pieces (a race war dust up in a bar with a drag queen and little person comes to mind), *Mr. No Legs* keeps a nice pace, even rewarding the viewer with a gratuitous, 10-minute car chase at the end. And I mean gratuitous literally: the plot has wrapped up completely before the chase begins, rendering the entire affair meaningless. But then again, who am I to complain about superfluous shit?

White Fire

| 1984 | Turkey, France, United States | Dir. Jean-Marie Pallardy |

An American-Turkish-French-Italian co-production, *White Fire* has American stars, the aesthetics of Italian exploitation, a Turkish setting, and the weird sexuality of the French new wave. There's a lot to recommend—especially a cheesy 80s theme song and Fred Williamson in a rare villain role—but you come to this film for one thing and one thing only: the complete, unadulterated incest vibes.

Siblings Bo and Ingrid (Robert Ginty and Belinda Mayne) are orphaned at a young age and taken in by Sam (Jess Hahn), a local criminal who raises them to be jewel thieves. Ingrid works at a diamond mine that has the same uniform and office décor as the Death Star, when her boss uncovers the legendary (and very radioactive) White Fire diamond, setting off a chain of events that leads to her death. Which devastates Bo, because you see, he really loves her. Like, really *really* loves her.

Bo is the type of brother who steals his naked sister's towel, ogles, and then says things like, "If only you weren't my sister." Therefore, when she dies, and he can't see her naked anymore, he enters a downward spiral. That is, until he meets Olga (Diana Goodman), a near dead ringer for his sister—"near" being the operative word. In order to carry out the theft of the White Fire, Bo makes Olga undergo plastic surgery to look just like Ingrid.

And if you're thinking it, yes! Belinda Mayne returns to the role of Fake Ingrid, as Bo falls in love with her. We are treated to love montage after love montage. Kissing, caressing, nudity. It's wild, eye-popping stuff.

There's also action and stuff.

Avenging Force

| 1986 | United States | Dir. Sam Firstenberg |

Avenging Force is the sequel to Cannon Film's *Invasion U.S.A* (1985), this time with Michael Dudikoff in the role of Matt Hunter after Chuck Norris turned it down. Dudikoff was fresh off *American Ninja* (1985), where he single-handedly popularized ninjas in American culture. (If you were alive in the 80s, you know exactly I'm talking about.)

Hunter, now retired, lives with his sister and grandfather on a farm in Louisiana. In addition to being the best solider and Secret Service agent on the planet, he's also incredibly skilled at lassoing bulls on horseback. However, his farmhand dexterity is no match for the plot, for he and his family must travel to New Orleans to hang with Larry Richards (Steve James), an old war buddy running for U.S. Senator.

After a lovely dinner, the two families head to a Mardi Gras parade, where Richards mans a float with his children. There, gunmen from John P. Ryan's white supremacist terrorist organization, the Pentangle, open fire, killing Richards' young son. Hunter and Richards, not surprisingly, embark on a violent and bonkers journey of revenge, utilizing every technique Uncle Sam taught them.

Fact: there is nothing finer on earth than John P. Ryan chewing the scenery as a villain in a Cannon film (for further proof, check out *Death Wish 4*). Despite how cartoonish and heightened his role is in *Avenging*

Force, Ryan emanates class in every frame. Hell, by the film's end, even I wanted to abandon every decent belief I hold about humanity and join his hunting club.

That's right. The Pentangle has a hunting club, where they hunt. . .men. The wonderful cold open features two men being chased through the swamp by a guy in a white slasher mask wielding a samurai sword, all before one of them is speared with a trident by a large man sporting an old school executioner's mask.

It might be the New Orleans locale or *The Most Dangerous Game* element, but *Avenging Force* provides the same sweaty, cocaine head rush of *Hard Target* (1993) in that there's a raucous, okay-I-guess-we're-doing-this-now kinda vibe. One could easily imagine Jean-Claude Van Damme walking into any scene and punching a snake in the face.

Though Sam Firstenberg is most known for directing *American Ninja* and *Revenge of the Ninja* (1983), this is by far his best work. Cannon being Cannon, you're going to get the clunky stuff, stilted dialogue, and weak character work, but Firstenberg takes the $4.7 million budget he has and creates what feels like a gigantic film. The action set pieces are huge and the scope epic. There's a scene towards the end when Dudikoff comes up on a rural Cajun community, and it's shot just like the scene at the end of Walter Hill's *Southern Comfort* (1981). Indeed, *Avenging Force* possesses a grounded quality lacking in its Cannon cousins.

Dangerous Men

| 2005 | United States | Dir. Jahangir Salehi Yeganehrad |

The 2005 release date is a bit misleading. Jahangir Salehi Yeganehrad, an Iranian immigrant who bills himself as John S. Rad, began work on *Dangerous Men* in 1984, a fact that becomes immediately clear once the film starts, and you're hypnotized by the high hair and constant Casio keyboard loops. Eighty minutes later, when the credits roll and you regain consciousness, watch out. The phrase "Black Pepper" will activate you *Naked Gun*-style, and you'll spend an entire afternoon Googling "senator" and "public appearance."

Which is where it derives its title. *Dangerous Men* is an indoctrination video à la *The Parallax View*, a weaponized form of independent cinema manufactured to decimate the global body politik. Rad premiered his first cut in 1985, but the CIA shut it down after the first screening, forcing the director back into the underground, where he spent the next 24 years perfecting the film, before the anarcho terrorists over at Drafthouse Films picked it up for distribution—and thereby ensuring the worldwide economic collapse. (This is also why Yeganehrad had to change his name to Rad, as to evade the unending parade of G-Men hot on his trail.)

Since Drafthouse Films released the film properly in 2015, currency no longer exists and capital wealth is determined by how many human rib cages you have stored in your garage. Folks toil in their bunks at the camps, reminiscing back to when they were one of like 40 people who saw *Dangerous Men* during its stint at five Los Angeles theaters in 2005. They would happily dish out twelve rib cages for the pristine Blu-ray, if they weren't now—at the threat of being whipped—grinding human bone into a malleable puddy to build shrines.

The film's plot, only decipherable after nine sessions of hypnotherapy, plays like a loose crime anthology, something akin to 2018's *Low Life*. Characters appear and disappear with the frivolousness of life here in Red Sector Four (I type slow and softly; one of Daegon's drones was nearby mere moments ago). But the core of the story centers around Mina, whose fiancé is murdered by rapey bikers. She goes full *Ms. 45* and enacts a one-woman war on all men, utilizing a knife he keeps hidden in the crack of her butt. Real Pam Grier gun-in-the-fro energy there.

Then Mina's arc sorta fizzles out, and we follow her would-be brother-in-law, Police Detective, as he tracks down biker gang kingpin, Black Pepper, a man he suspects to be involved in his brother's murder. This subplot waxes nostalgic, in that it reminds us of a time when justice wasn't meted out by roving, pipe-wielding vigilante gangs. It's a warm, inspiring feeling one can only get hunched over a good barrel fire. Nevertheless, that emotion is fleeting; the film switches gears again in the final third, focusing on a group of characters we haven't met up that point and just ends.

For a movie that's caused immense, global suffering and countless genocides, it's fairly unusual. In one sequence, Mina is hitchhiking and picked up by a squirrely British man who attempts to rape her. She turns the tables and steals his truck, leaving him alone and naked in the middle of the desert. For most films, this would be the end of that man's storyline. But Dangerous Men doesn't operate that way. We spend the next FIVE AND A HALF MINUTES with this dude as he walks, cries, sings, and dances across the landscape, hiding his privates with desert brush.

At this point, we begin to suspect the filmmaker's insidious motive and point of view. Rad is portraying a world filled with evil men who leave nothing but misery and violence in their wake. They are a menace to be destroyed and tortured—which is something you just don't posit in this day and age. Do you know how rare sperm is? The last guy in my neighborhood with swimmers lived like a king for two months until Daegon found out. Let's just say he now plays soprano in his barbershop quartet, if you catch my drift.

Yet, for that particular untimeliness, Rad's work is singular and unique and one-of-a-kind. (I apologize for the redundancy. The average intelligence dropped considerably once we started milking microplastics for water.) *Dangerous Men* functions both as pure amateurishness and at a level most modern art can't achieve, solely due to a studio system that weeds out the creative and weird. Oh shit, the drone's back. Just gotta, uh—

○ ○ ○

DIRECTOR SPOTLIGHT:
Andy Sidaris

*"Most importantly, **my pictures are not mean-spirited**. So many movies are! I do not allow profanity in our movies. I do not put our women in compromising situations where blood and guts are graphically shown. I maintain a dignity for our actors and insist they have a sense of humor in their performances. No one else does this!"*
– Andy Sidaris from *Bullets Bombs and Babes: The Films of Andy Sidaris*

To hear Andy Sidaris tell it, his films are a gentleman's affair, works operating with a chivalric code and upmost respect for the fairer sex. And compared to similar exploitation fare, the director might have a point. There are no gratuitous rape scenes, the women are positive about their bodies and sexualities, and if a man dares take advantage, he is swiftly punished—usually with a powerful explosive.

But let's not go nuts. Sidaris made a very particular kind of movie, and he made it over and over again. Connoisseurs of late-night cable programming from the 80s and 90s refer to this type of film as a "Triple B": Bullets, Bombs, and Babes (or Boobs, if you like to party). At its core, a "Triple B" film is a collection of soft-core pornography vignettes wrapped inside a no-frills action story. The acting, done mostly by *Playboy* Playmates and soap actors, serves merely as a recitation of the script, filler to get us from A to B, explosion to Boob City.

I say this with no intention of cheapening Sidaris' filmography. While his films adhered to a precise and exploitative formula, he never shied away from big, creative swings within that framework. He operated cheap and fast, far outside the studio system and forged products of immense personality relative to the budget. Bottom line: you know when you're watching an Andy Sidaris film.

Stacey

| 1973 | United States | Dir. Andy Sidaris |

Before crossing over into film, Sidaris made a name for himself revolutionizing the way we watch football. As a broadcast director for professional and college games, he added more cameras for multiple coverage angles, allowing for closeups on the sidelines, which turned the coaches and players into characters of the overall spectacle. He even invented the leering camera zooms on the cheerleaders we take for granted today, a technique dubbed the "honey shot."

Sidaris spent the 60s and 70s directing sports for the major networks, most notably the Olympics and *ABC's Wide World of Sports*. Leveraging his experience shooting professional motorsports, Sidaris directed the documentary, *The Racing Scene* in 1969. The doc follows James Garner's foray into Formula One racing after he caught the bug filming John Frankenheimer's *Grand Prix* (1966). All but forgotten today, *The Racing Scene* is one of the best sports documentaries ever made and very instructive as to the direction of Sidaris' early filmography. (You can certainly bet the film offers a shot or two of Miss Continental Racing Queen Majken Kruse.)

In 1973, Sidaris partnered with Roger Corman to direct his narrative feature debut, *Stacey*, a creative leap that connected the technical expertise of his past with the exploitation tendencies that would define his future. The first minute of the film illustrates this perfectly. Opening with a Formula One car zipping around a track (presumably stock footage Sidaris had collected over the years), the driver eventually exits to the locker room. Once the helmet comes off, we learn the driver is Playmate Anne Randall (May 1967), and without missing a beat, we freezeframe on her bare breasts and title card.

This is Stacey Hanson. A private eye with a race car side hustle, Hanson is hired by wealthy matriarch Florence Chambers (Marjorie Bennett) to investigate her three children, an effort to determine which one deserves to inherit the family fortune. Hanson integrates herself into the daily matters of the family and uncovers a twisty plot that spares no amount of sleaze.

Hindsight being what it is, it's easy to pinpoint some of the style and flourishes that would become staples of the Sidaris canon: a strong-willed and competent female protagonist, soft-core aesthetic, and ambitious set pieces shot lean and mean. However, at this point in his career, Sidaris hasn't fully developed his unique film language, and the movie plays indistinguishably from Corman's other 70s exploitation output.

Seven

| 1979 | United States | Dir. Andy Sidaris |

Sidaris continued to work in television throughout the production of his first several films, even flying back and forth between movie projects in Hawaii and sporting events on the mainland. In fact, Hawaii would become home base for all future Sidaris productions, the first one being *Seven*.

Starring William Smith, *Seven* adds the next layer of the "Triple B" formula, that of a likable team of (mostly) beautiful characters taking on a vast criminal conspiracy. The U.S. government comes a-knockin' to world-renowned mercenary Drew Sevano (Smith), following a string of high-level assassinations of American politicians and diplomats.

Agreeing to take on the job for SEVEN million dollars, SEVano assembles a team of SEVEN mercenaries to track down the assassins and foil their plans.

If *Stacey* were a hint of where things would go, *Seven* is the system locking into place. The goofy, middle school-level humor. *Playboy* Playmates popping their tops. An unnecessarily complex, James Bond-esque storyline. Though the film does not share the same universe of all subsequent Sidaris projects, it may as well.

Malibu Express

| 1985 | United States | Dir. Andy Sidaris |

Then, in 1985, it's off to the races. Literally. Sidaris remakes *Stacey* as *Malibu Express*, this time splitting the race car driving private detective lead role into two. Darby Hinton plays Cody Abilene, the yacht club-living, playboy P.I. and Playmate Lynda Wiesmeier takes over driving duties as Cody's car racing friend, June Khnockers. The story is identical, but Sidaris ups the ante by throwing in a side plot about traitor Americans selling tech secrets to the Russians.

Malibu Express also marks the beginning of the shared universe called the "Triple B Series" or the "L.E.T.H.A.L. Ladies Series." From here on out, almost every Sidaris-directed effort will feature an Abilene cousin as a top-notch government agent, whose joke (like Cody) is that he can't shoot for shit. The vast array of additional characters will begin to overshadow the Abilenes in the series, but they are the lynchpin that holds everything together.

The film is important, too, because it's the first one Sidaris owned outright. This was a major source of pride for him. No longer beholden to the whims of shady investors and producers, Sidaris and his wife (and producer), Arlene, retained ownership of all future films by completely funding the projects themselves. Arlene is quoted in Sidaris' autobiography, *Bullets Bombs and Babes: The Films of Andy Sidaris*, saying:

> It didn't take me long to become accustomed to the importance of every decision and the satisfaction of the two of us being able to fulfill our vision in filmmaking. Unlike a studio, we can

make instant decisions. The good news is if we need to spend a thousand dollars we can do it on the spot. The bad news is, it's *our* thousand dollars!

Hard Ticket to Hawaii
| 1987 | United States | Dir. Andy Sidaris |

Enter: Dona Spier and Hope Marie Carlton. March 1984 and July 1985 (respectively). The bombshell duo headlined three Sidaris films together, with Spier doing a total of seven. *Hard Ticket to Hawaii*, their first pairing, introduces their series characters, Donna (Spier) and Taryn (Carlton) as

Ron Moss as Rowdy Abilene in *Hard Ticket to Hawaii*.
Photo Courtesy of Arlene Sidaris and Malibu Bay Films.

pilots for Molokai Cargo, a transport service. Donna is an undercover DEA agent and looks after Taryn, who is in witness protection.

Things go south after they lose track of a mutated, giant snake they are transporting, while also uncovering a diamond smuggling operation on the island. And yes, you heard that correctly. Do those two threads (snake and diamond smuggling) have anything to do with one another? Does one affect the other? No. Not at all. But we are in the hands of a master.

In essence, *Hard Ticket to Hawaii* is two films: a sexploitation actioner and bonkers animal attacks movie. It also contains my favorite Andy Sidaris scene of all time.

Rowdy Abilene (Ron Moss) and Jade (Harold Diamond) drive down a deserted beach road. An assassin on a skateboard coasts down a hill with a blowup sex doll held up to shield the sight of his gun. As he approaches, the assassin throws the sex doll and opens fire, hitting Jade. Rowdy then backs the vehicle up, knocking the assailant into the air and shoots him with a bazooka like a clay pigeon. Then, before the sex doll hits the ground, Rowdy blows it out of the sky.

Do or Die

| 1991 | United States | Dir. Andy Sidaris |

Spier and Carlton reprise their roles in *Picasso Trigger* (1988) and *Savage Beach* (1989), before the Taryn character is replaced by Nicole Justin in *Do or Die*, played by Roberta Vasquez (November 1984). Having one of Sidaris' more lean plots, the 1991 film sees the introduction of recurring villain Kane, who, for sport, sends six squads of assassins to kill Donna and Nicole. That's it. That's the story.

(Strangely, Kane is played by veteran Japanese actor Pat Morita in *Do or Die*, but in later installments, such as *Hard Hunted* [1992] and *Fit to Kill* [1993], the character is portrayed by the very white Geoffrey Moore, sporting a British accent. Hence, it should probably go without saying that if these films were made in the Marvel era, fanboys would aneurism their gourds off.)

Do or Die is also the second Sidaris outing for Erik Estrada (Ponch from *CHiPs*). Estrada plays the villain in the previous *Guns* (1990), but returns here as different character, an Air Force officer who wields

Dona Spier and Roberta Vasquez in *Do or Die*. Photo courtesy of Arlene Sidaris and Malibu Bay Films.

exploding baseballs. No joke. In one scene, as Estrada is pinned behind a tree by a gunman, he randomly pulls baseball after baseball from his pants pocket and hurls them at the bad guy. And trust me, that dude is just as confused as we are. Then, the final baseball has a red button on it; Estrada pushes it before lobbing it at the gunman—who uses his gun like a bat to hit it. Boom!

That is the type of odd humor that has endeared Sidaris to a legion of direct-to-video VHS aficionados over the years. He went on to direct four more films after *Do or Die*, not adjusting his formula one iota, and ended his run in 1998 with *L.E.T.H.A.L. Ladies: Return to Savage Beach*. He even wrote and produced two films that his son Christian directed, *Enemy Gold* (1993) and *The Dallas Connection* (1994).

At a casual distance, it might seem easy to lump Sidaris' output in with the rest of the Skinemax programming of the era. But as stupid as it sounds, there is a kind of wholesomeness at the heart of the sleaze he puts onscreen. Where a lot of porn purposefully engages you on a tactile level—you know, to get you going—there is a larger-than-life quality to the way Sidaris shoots his babes and studs. It puts you at a distance, and you feel these beautiful, perfectly sculped people are untouchable. That elevates the action and the heroics, which in turn, makes a Sidaris production stand apart from its late-night compatriots. Throw in a little self-aware humor, and it becomes a genre all of its own.

○ ○ ○

Rolling Vengeance
| 1987 | Canada | Dir. Steven Hilliard Stern |

Though it was likely one of the last productions under the Canadian tax shelter, *Rolling Vengeance* shares a kinship with all the Canuxploitation films that came before.

In 1974, the Canadian government, in an attempt to jumpstart their fledgling film industry, allowed financiers to deduct the entirety of their production costs for films made in-country. The deduction was reduced to 50% in 1982 and reset to the original 30% in 1987. This fertile playground birthed directors like David Cronenberg, Ivan Reitman, and Bob Clark, as well as becoming a mecca for shameless American producers looking to abuse the tax haven. The films of this era consist of similar elements and themes, such as geographic isolation, blue collar characters, the indifference of the natural world, body horror—and, of course, pure, unsullied politeness.

And *Rolling Vengeance* has the distinction of being the politest revenge film ever made.

Don Michael Paul stars as Joey Rosso, a young man running a trucking company with his father (Lawrence Dane from *Scanners*). But this is really Ned Beatty's show. He plays Tiny Doyle, a tooth-missin', shady AF strip club/used car dealership owner (both located in the same parking lot, naturally). He's also the backwoods patriarch of five degenerate, cartoonishly evil sons, who help run the family business and commit general mischief and murder all over town.

Everyone else in the film is just the most pleasant, down-to-earth people you've ever met; people you'd never want anything bad to happen to. And nothing ever does.

Just kidding. One afternoon, Joey's mother is driving with all the younger siblings (*awkwardly* young compared to the rest of the family), and they encounter the Doyle brothers in their truck, drunk as skunks. The boys terrorize the family, eventually forcing the car into an oncoming semi-truck, killing everyone.

This being a revenge film and all, the Doyles only receive a slap on the wrist from the judge and are free to go. And yeah, so now you're thinking: are we ready for some badass monster truck justice served cold as a frosty, Alberta morning? Nope, not at all. The film settles back down into a family melodrama, and people continue being really, really nice.

It's at this point one begins to wonder if it's even possible for *Rolling Vengeance* to go as dark as something like *Death Wish* (1974) or *Rolling Thunder* (1977). Joey's just way too nice of a guy to smoke a bunch of fools, right? Well, fret not. One thing leads to another and another, of which finally pushes Joey into building a custom monster truck killing machine out of spare junkyard parts. A true wonder to behold.

Once the truck enters about halfway through, we're off to the races. Monster trucks were all the rage in the 80s and 90s, and the film finds every opportunity to exploit the twelve-year-old imagination in each of us (you may recall something about a used car lot somewhere above). The writers are fully aware of Chekhov's rule that if a giant drill on the hood of a monster truck is introduced in the second act, it must be used to pulverize hicks.

Overall, the tone of *Rolling Vengeance* is inconsistent, but it's not a dealbreaker. The running time is short and sweet (90 minutes), and Ned Beatty's hammed up performance negates anything bad you could possibly say. Throw in a cheese-tastic, Survivor-like soundtrack, and you'll be prepared to let this "monster trucker-piece" run all over you.

Okay, that last pun doesn't really work.

Live Like a Cop, Die Like a Man

| 1976 | Italy | Dir. Ruggero Deodato |

As the spaghetti western acquiesced to the law of diminishing returns in the early 70s, Italian filmmakers began looking elsewhere for inspiration. The American new wave was churning out popular cop and crime films, such as *The French Connection* (1971), *Dirty Harry* (1971), and *The Godfather* (1972), while the exploitation underbelly saw such vigilante ditties as *Death Wish* (1974) and *Coffy* (1973). In France, Jean-Pierre Melville had already put forth his crime masterpieces (and Michael Mann crib sheets), *Le Samouraï* (1967) and *Le Cercle Rouge* (1970). Which is all the long way of saying that, true to form, the Italians also wanted in on the action. Thus, the *poliziotteschi* genre came into being.

Or *Poliziesco all'Italiana*, if you're a real prick about your Italian grammar.

Poliziotteschi would prove to be the Italian film industry's most dominant genre for much of the decade of the 1970s, where established spaghetti western stars, such as Tomas Milian, Franco Nero, and Lee Van Cleef reigned almost as ubiquitously as before. The films were styled much like their American counterparts, incorporating all the same elements you would expect in run-of-the-mill crime, mob, cop, heist, and vigilante films. However, Italy was not a well nation at this point. The nation was in the midst of a two-decade long period of sociopolitical unrest (the "Years of Lead"). Crime and terrorism ran rampant; political parties openly engaged in assassinations, kidnappings, and bombings; organized crime families warred with each other on the streets; the deep, ingrained currant of fascism still flowed freely through the political climate, even in the post-Mussolini years. Hence, it's not surprising at all that a lot of this angst and violence found its way onto celluoid.

Bringing me to *Live Like a Cop, Die Like a Man*, one of the most fascistic, sexist, and...*coolest* things I've ever seen.

Directed by Ruggero Deodato (*Cannibal Holocaust*) and written by *poliziotteschi* legend Fernando Di Leo (*Il Boss*), the film is a reimagining of *Starsky & Hutch* by way of *Dirty Harry*. Marc Porel and Ray Lovelock play Fred and Tony, two vicious cops on the Special Force, a secretive police group that targets big criminals and whose own dirty deeds are swept under the rug by their chief (Adolfo Celi from *Thunderball*). Though the central plot involves taking down a mob kingpin named Bibi (Renato Salvatori), much of the action comes from unrelated interludes, as Fred and Tony intervene in things like a hostage situation, robbery, and badass motorcycle chase for no real reason.

Live Like a Cop, Die Like a Man exudes style and cool in equal measure, dulling some of the film's more reprehensible aspects. I'm particularly partial to the soundtrack, which consists of two Bob Dylan-ish folk songs sung by Lovelock himself ("Won't Take Too Long" and "Maggie"). On paper, the contrast between that style of music and the violence on-screen probably sounds anachronistic, though in practice, it lends the film a greater quality worth discussing: that of the characters' resonance as folk heroes.

I imagine in those dark days in Italy, the average movie goer would get much satisfaction in watching these hip, young cops blast away seedy criminals—no matter how fascistic or inappropriate their tactics are. The American parallel is most certainly the success of *Death Wish* in 1974.

Americans, too, were exhausted by the crime in cities such as New York and L.A., which had reached absurd levels we haven't seen since, and audiences were more than delighted to see Charles Bronson take on the criminal element by extrajudicial means.

And that, to me, is where I find *Live Like a Cop, Die Like a Man* slightly off-putting. There's no denying the fascistic, extreme right wing themes in both, *Death Wish* and *Dirty Harry*. However, both films deal with those issues in very complex and moral ways. Liberal audiences are often appalled at the pro-gun, fascistic message in *Death Wish*, but never seem to mention or notice the complexity of the entire message (as far as director Michael Winner would ever have a message). Gun culture is roundly mocked during the wild west, touristy cowboy reenactment—not to mention, Bronson even jokes at one point that a gun is only an extension of one's penis. By the end, Paul Kersey is a raging psychopath, a hollowed-out husk of a man whose only identity is that of a vigilante and murderer. It's a tragedy and not anything to be celebrated.

Live Like a Cop, Die Like a Man offers none of these complexities. These guys are just fascist dickweeds and serial harassers of women, which admittedly, chips away at some of the enjoyment of the film. But when you watch Fred and Tony practice their shooting skills by lining up cans along the sides of a canyon, before spinning around ceaselessly, dizzily shooting at the cans inches from each other's heads—you're a bit more forgiving of fascism.

Casus Kiran

| 1968 | Turkey | Dir. Yilmaz Atadeniz |

While I assume the majority of people alive right now have never seen or heard of a film serial, they without a doubt know the genre's many tropes and structures, even if they aren't aware of it. The character of Indiana Jones, for example, was George Lucas' attempt at replicating the serials of old with a more adult, contemporary aesthetic. And any weirdo who's seen *Raiders of the Lost Ark* (1981) less than three hundred times has the mechanics of the serial inculcated into their soul: a masculine strongman hero, exotic locales, loads of gun violence and fisticuffs, Nazis, and spunky women who always find themselves in danger. Let us not forget, of course, endless deus ex machinas.

(The plural of deus ex machina is actually dei ex machina, but one would have to be a real gutter douchebag to just drop that one in there without comment.)

(And since I commented, and therefore brought attention to it and myself, I am definitively not a douchebag or the equivalent of genital psoriasis.)

Where was I? Oh yes, serials. Generally, it's best to think of the serial format as the first television programming. They've been around as long as film itself, but their heyday—and period in which the structures we recognize solidified—ran from the 30s to the early 50s. These were the quaint times when a Saturday trip to the theater yielded more than just cinema. You had a newsreel, cartoon, previews, and that week's serial, all before the movie started.

Featuring characters like Captain Marvel, Flash Gordon, Batman, Zorro, Green Hornet, The Phantom, and Dick Tracy, the serials (as the name suggests) were bigger stories broken into smaller, episodic installments around 20 minutes in length. Each title ran weekly for about 15 episodes, while each chapter began with a recap from the week prior and ended on a cliffhanger with our hero in peril. All the major studios such as Universal and Columbia had their mittens in the serial game, but Republic, a much smaller outfit that only produced serials, is most associated with the genre today, primarily for their takes on Captain Marvel and The Lone Ranger.

And that would be the end of the story, if it weren't for Turkey. Similar to the aliens in *Contact* (1997) sending our television signals back at us, the Turks fell in love with American serials and beamed them back to the rest of humanity. The instigator of the serial subgenre in Turkey was Yilmaz Atadeniz, who in 1967, kicked everything off with *Kilink Istanbul'da*, an intentional throwback to those weekly American stories, showcasing a flying superhero named Superman. (Anyone familiar with Turkish cinema in the slightest knows existing copyrights are more of a feature than a bug.)

Atadeniz returned a year later with virtually the same cast, directing *Casus Kiran*, which took its hero's name straight from the Republic serial, *Spy Smasher* (1942). Except where American Spy Smasher has a cool ass vehicle called the Gyrosub, Turkish Spy Smasher has a motorcycle. The Gyrosub, at a moment's notice, could be an airplane, car, or submarine. Turkish Spy Smasher's motorcycle is just. . .a motorcycle. Though, presumably, he could use it to go buy some gyros.

The masked, Batman-esque hero is played by Irfan Atasoy, who played Superman in Atadeniz's prior film. His sidekick and lover Sevda (Sevda Ferda) is the daughter of Detective Cavit, the Commissioner Gordon of the piece and Spy Smasher's supposed friend inside the police department. Together, they attempt to foil the dastardly plans of the Mask, whose plans are so dastardly that I can't even really understand or follow them. But they're bad, believe me!

Casus Kiran moves like lightning, much like a full-length serial without the chapter breaks. Atadeniz, in true serial fashion, indulges in fistfight after fistfight and lets each action sequence flow into the next, with only quick interludes to see what the Mask and his henchmen are up to. The film doesn't come to a complete stop like its American brethren, but it does allow for Spy Smasher to get into the same sticky situations, only to be rescued by well-placed dei ex machina.

Whether you're a serial aficionado or just being introduced to the genre, *Casus Kiran* offers a great return on your investment, should you crave a mindless action spectacle. (And you'd have to be a real douchebag not to want that.)

○ ○ ○

BONUS INTERVIEW
Arlene Sidaris

Arlene Sidaris was the wife of the late Andy Sidaris and producer on all his films, beginning with Hard Ticket to Hawaii *(1987). She is currently working on an updated version of Andy's autobiography,* Bullets Bombs and Babes: The Films of Andy Sidaris, *due out in 2022.*

Matt Rotman: Andy wrote in [*Bullets Bombs and Babes: The Films of Andy Sidaris*] that you helped immensely with the scriptwriting—that he would write really quickly and then you'd polish it up. What were the scripts like when you got them? What kind of reworkings/revisions were doing?

Arlene Sidaris: Andy wrote like he spoke: fast and furious. I am quite the opposite. If he wrote a scene highlighting the action, I would be sure that the action he intended was on the paper. That diligence could affect the props, wardrobe, time of day and actors in the scene.

MR: Andy also bragged that you kept every project on or under budget. All of these films have pretty big set pieces/explosions, etc. What were some of the strategies you incorporated in managing the budget?

AS: My strategy was to do a budget for the first draft, suggest changes to accommodate our target budget and revise as revisions were written.

MR: When Andy was still doing sports broadcasting and flying back and forth between projects and raising a family at the same time—what was this time period like? How did you guys get through it?

AS: It was definitely a challenge. There was one period when Mike Friedman, a fantastic cameraman Andy worked with at ABC, took over. It was only for a few days but he did a great job.

MR: Besides the obvious financial benefits, what's the best part about owning your films outright?

AS: We only had to answer to each other. We put our home up as collateral, so the jeopardy was great, but I didn't have to get approval if I wanted to spend $1,000. The issue was: it was my $1,000.

MR: What kind of items are being updated in the book, and why?

AS: The book will incorporate activities of the product since the original issues, such as streaming, worldwide theatrical exhibition, including Q&A with the audience from my desktop computer in Beverly Hills, 1,000-piece puzzle, music from *Hard Ticket to Hawaii* on vinyl, an upcoming DVD version of *Hard Ticket to Hawaii* due out soon. There will be tributes to the people we've lost, Julie Strain and Rodrigo Obregon, and tributes to Andy by some significant people in his life. 1`

Interview conducted September 7, 2021 by email.

Slashers 6

ASK FIVE DIFFERENT horror fans what the first slasher film was, and you're bound to get five different answers. Was it *Psycho* (1960)? How about *Black Christmas* (1974)? Maybe even Mario Bava's *A Bay of Blood* (1971)?

Oh, I can feel your brains vibrating from here: "Okay, Mr. Smarty-Pants, tell us then. What was the first slasher film?" That's easy. *I Still Know What You Did Last Summer* (1998), when Mekhi Phifer cut out all of our hearts.

Okay, next question, you adorable assortment of vibrating brains.

All facetiousness aside, my opinion tends toward a more traditional view of things—starting with those years we technically refer to as the early 80s (as *The Years of Fucking and Sucking* is already the name of Pat Boone's autobiography). The slasher cycle kicked off in 1980 with *Friday the 13th*, when everyone from the major studios to your uncle no one talks about anymore seized the opportunity to replicate the *Friday* formula. With Paramount Pictures literally printing money (having bought the distribution rights to Sean S. Cunningham's film for pennies), the other studios followed suit, buying up anything with tits, blood, and a psycho killer. This also coincided with the birth of the VHS market, which made it even easier for indie film producers to bypass the studio system altogether, being that they could just sell their product straight to the video rental stores.

Okay, vibrating brains. I hear you. Yes, I know *Friday the 13th* was just a cash grab after the success of *Halloween* (1978). But the terrible, war-like metaphor I always use is: if *Halloween* was the grenade of the slasher cycle, then *Friday the 13th* is what pulled the pin. The tropes we associate with the standard stalk-and-slash begin with Cunningham's film and are then solidified with *Halloween II*. More importantly, though, the economy that drove the slasher era did not begin in earnest until after the release of *Friday the 13th*.

Despite the fact that we generally designate the years 1980 to 1983 as the slasher cycle, the resilient genre has hacked and sawed its way into the modern era, and I've devised this chapter to reflect this particular stubbornness. (Stabbernness?) We will touch upon the overlooked gems of the initial wave, but since this is my favorite genre, it is important to me to highlight the strides and creativity—and basic batshittery—of latter slasher films, as well. I do all of this knowing full well that the slasher film peaked with Gus Van Sant's *Psycho* remake in 1998.

Easter Bunny, Kill! Kill!

| 2006 | United States | Dir. Chad Ferrin |

Not as family friendly as the title would suggest, Chad Ferrin's *Easter Bunny, Kill! Kill!* is bargain basement grime of the highest order. Ferrin, a product of the Troma system, imbues his film with that company's patented classlessness and tawdry charm, but his unshakeable confidence as a director furnishes the movie an identity of its own. The experience is one of watching sleaze itself melt and ooze onto the frames of a Lifetime movie, big ole globules of gunk like butter inside Grammy's sweet holiday rolls.

At its core, *Easter Bunny, Kill! Kill!* is a heartwarming mother-son story. Mindy Peters (Charlotte Marie) is a single mom and nurse trying to make ends meet and care for her special needs son, Nicholas, who suffers from mentally retarded cerebral palsy (MRCP). Things take a turn for the bloody when Mindy, having to work a double shift on Easter Sunday, enlists her criminal boyfriend Remington (Timothy Muskatell) to look after Nicholas. Remington wastes no time whoring out the young boy to a local pedophile for cocaine and hookers, but events spiral out of control once a bunny-masked killer starts stalking and slashing the lowlife house guests one by one.

Ferrin pulls no punches illustrating how depraved and despicable Remington and his cohorts are—which, yes, makes scenes of Remington verbally abusing Nicholas hard to stomach, but the grisly, satisfying payoff of the murders is your reward for sitting through it. And I can tell you from my personal experience screening hundreds of cheap slashers in a festival setting that they all tend to blur together eventually, only existing as a kind of lumpy collective memory in your brain. There is a weird humanity within the mean streak of *Easter Bunny Kill! Kill!* that will linger very distinctly long after you've watched it.

Bosque de Muerte
| 1993 | Mexico | Dir. Carlos David Ortigoza |

Poachers don't stand a chance. Not against Jaguar.

Bosque de Muerte opens—rather anachronistically for a slasher film—like a coked up Greenpeace commercial. As loggers illegally harvest trees in a forest reserve, shots ring out, dropping several of them before the others can find shelter. A voice calls from the brush a delayed warning that this is protected land. Meet Jaguar (Jorge Reyonoso), the most committed forest ranger on the planet.

Cut to the more standard slasher opening: a van full of youngsters winds the curves of an isolated highway, overheating and smoking from the hood. Pulling over in search of anti-freeze, the group encounters Jaguar, who has the wounded contingent of the ambushed logging party in the back of his pickup. When the police arrive to arrest and take away the men, Jaguar politely reminds the officers to collect the bottom-half of a leg he shot off.

He then gives our future victims a bottle of anti-freeze.

Our corpses-in-wait are an agreeable sort, college-aged men and women all horned up and heading to a cabin for a weekend getaway. This "cabin" turns out to be the sprawling estate owned by the father of Sylvia, one of the "teens" played by 43-year-old actor Alejandra Espejo. An age that should give hope to all older, would-be murder victims out there.

The estate holds bad vibes for Sylvia, whose mother went missing in the lake years ago. Unfortunately for her, the trauma returns when a member of their clan, Adolfo, vanishes while snorkeling in the same lake. (Fun fact: Adolfo is played by Andrés García Jr., son of Mexican megastar Andrés García.) In true slasher fashion, the group splits up; Sylvia and her boyfriend go looking for Jaguar to aid in the search for their friend, while the rest stay at the house—prime pickins' for any crazed madman wishing to inflict some heavily clichéd carnage on our unsuspecting horndogs.

This is the point in the review where I am legally obligated to tell you that this is 60 minutes into an 80-minute film. Rest assured the remaining 20 minutes do offer up the traditional stalk-and-slash goodies, but to get here, we've just spent an hour hanging out with these yahoos as they fuck, joke around, and fuck some more. And you know what? It doesn't hurt the film! Like the best slashers (*Black Christmas '74* and *The House on Sorority Row*), you enjoy being around these characters. They're dopey, but innocent, and you wait with patient dread for their demise.

The Mexican slasher boom followed the American cycle by seven or eight years, coming into its own with the Rubén Galindo Jr. films *Don't Panic* (1988) and *Grave Robbers* (1989). Hence, in 1993, when the Americans were a couple years away from turning the microscope inward with *Scream* (1996), our friends south of the border were still gleefully and earnestly churning out checklist slashers. *Bosque de Muerte* is no exception.

Remarkable, though, is that director Carlos David Ortigoza was 78 years old during production. Despite this—old director, old star, old genre—nothing feels tired or antiquated. Without a doubt, the film adheres to a formula that was almost 15 years old at that point, but Ortigoza proves that with great characters and a little weirdness, the slasher genre can be perennially relevant.

Kolobos

| 1999 | United States | Dir. Daniel Liatowitsch, Todd Ocvirk |

For better or worse, the post-*Scream* slasher phase of the late 90s and early 2000s had a particular vibe and aesthetic. From *I Know What You Did Last Summer* (1997) to *Urban Legend* (1998) to *Valentine* (2001), everything was hip, sleek, and subdued by the aw-shucks wholesomeness of a *Dawson's Creek* cast. Opinions of the era vary based on whether or not you were a teenager at the time, but there's no denying we are entering a period of reevaluation for these films as the Millennials wax nostalgic about their horror roots.

Despite this contemporary reappraisal, though, *Kolobos* remains as unappreciated now as the day it came out.

Faceless having fun out there. Photo courtesy of Edward R. Taylor and Armitage Pictures.

That's partly because it's a weird fucking film. Furthermore, it was marketed as a straight-ahead slasher movie in the year of *Blair Witch*, when studio horror was in the awkward transition to more supernatural offerings. An on-the-nose throwback to the days of Dario Argento and Lucio Fulci, *Kolobos* just didn't have a home, even with its meta, *Scream*-esque observations.

Directed by Daniel Liatowitsch and Todd Ocvirk, the film opens in a dreamy stream of consciousness. We experience the world through the eyes of someone stumbling through a city alleyway. After being struck by an oncoming car, the audience is transported to the hospital, where the doctors and police detectives ask us who we are and what happened.

Kolobos, then, becomes a story about how we got here. The hospital patient is an artist named Kyra (Amy Weber), one of five strangers in a *Real World*-like film experiment who each agree to live in a secluded house full of cameras. There's the shitty and immature standup comic, a pretentious actress, nerdy cinephile, and YOLO free spirit. All of them fodder—I mean stock characters—I mean, uh, let's go with people who say and do things.

When a character is soon killed by circular saw blades flying from the walls, the others attempt to flee the house, only to discover that metal covers are blocking the doors and windows. Now, with no escape, they must survive a sadistic maniac hunting them one by one. A hulking freak the film simply credits as Faceless, the killer devises a series of bloody traps and scenarios with a ghoulish proto-*Saw* flair.

This probably sounds fairly straight forward, and it is. However, as the film unfolds, so does its sanity. Kyra, our avatar into the story, loses her grip on reality, seeing things that may or not be real. And to boot, *Kolobos* offers no concrete answers by the time we get to the credits. Liatowitsch and Ocvirk are perfectly content to wallow in the nightmare logic of a Fulci film, filling the screen with Argento reds, greens, and blues. They even recreate the eyeball scene from *Zombi 2* (1979), while the theme song itself is about one note shy of plagiarizing Goblin's *Suspiria* (1977) theme.

Our current cultural moment is defined by the monetization of nostalgia, and it is rather easy to be turned off by throwback after throwback. But this is 1999! *Kolobos* came to the party two decades early, and no one knew what the fuck was going on. Hence, I'm hoping—if we must have a reevaluation of 90s slashers—folks wake to this film, as it is easily a top five slasher of that decade.

A Hora do Medo

| 1986 | Brazil | Dir. Francisco Cavalcanti |

The absolute worst question I've been asked during a job interview: "Is it ever okay to lie?" And me, not wanting to begin an employer-employee relationship on a lie, told the truth. "Yes."

For which, clerking for Clarence Thomas was never in the cards.

However, after watching *A Hora do Medo*, the Brazilian slasher film by Francisco Cavalcanti, I realized there is an even bigger red flag-raising question: "Do you have any relatives? Because you can't work here if you do." That's the query posed to Salvador while interviewing to be a driver for a wealthy family. Salvador's fiancé Eliana went missing working as the family's maid, and he is trying to *Parasite* his way in to unravel the mystery.

It turns out his instincts are honed, because this family, a mother and adult son combo, are a nasty bunch. Alberto, the son, is working out some childhood issues by violently murdering every young woman he sees. His mother, in turn, aids his murderous rampages by hiding the bodies and finding women to bring back to their isolated manor. (At one point, she shoots an abusive pimp with a poisoned dart *from the tip of an umbrella* and takes the prostitute home.)

Home being where the heart is buried, as they say. And in this case, I mean that literally. When Mommy isn't delighting herself in listening to her son have sex, she is taking trips to the makeshift vigil in the Back Forty, where she digs up her husband's skeleton for some… dirty bone?

Hence, *A Hora do Medo* does in 70 minutes what *Little House on the Prairie* spent nine seasons trying to accomplish.

Too sleazy to be *Psycho* (1960) and too in love with classical horror to be *Henry: Portrait of a Serial Killer* (1986), Cavalcanti's film feels more like *Maniac* (1980) by way of Michael Findlay. In fact, the Brazilian censors stripped the original cut of *A Hora do Medo* of most of its nudity, so legendary director José Mojica Marins (of Coffin Joe fame) came in and shot about ten minutes of additional gore. The padding is obvious (a lot time is spent dragging bodies around), but the movie's ultra-short length only serves to make this more endearing. Indeed, *A Hora do Medo* is so bare bones and streamlined that despite only having half of the English translation, I was never lost.

But then again, as a Jewish male, this is a home life I recognize.

Bits and Pieces

| 1985 | United States | Dir. Leland Thomas |

Piggybacking off *A Hora do Medo* (1986), here's another I'm-not-sexually-attracted-to-my-mommy-and-I'll-kill-every-woman-to-prove-it oddity that never left the 80s. The lone directing credit for Leland Thomas, *Bits and Pieces* only exists now outside the corporeal realm, forever destined as a digital bootleg due to the loss of the original negatives—perhaps to the relief of all involved. So I'm sure they'll appreciate me hyping it here.

S.E. Zygmont stars as Arthur, your everyday torture fetishist with a desire to impress a mannequin—I mean his dead mother. Little Arthur, as a child, spied on his mom having sex, got caught, and received the usual punishment: forced to wear a wig and makeup.

"A pervert, huh? Let's make him look like one," implores mom's boyfriend.

In no way growing up to be a pervert, Arthur spends his time outside male strip clubs hunting for sinful, young women to disembowel in front of Mommy Mannequin. One night, he crosses paths with Rosie (Suzanna Smith) and Tanya (Sheila Lussier), who are leaving the classy 2001 Club, faces beaming with the forbidden knowledge of Man Ass. Arthur kidnaps and murders Tanya, but becomes fixated on Rosie, as he believes she knows enough to bring him down.

Like *Pieces* (1982), a viewing of *Bits and Pieces* is an act of fermenting your mind grapes into a bitter, backwoods elixir. I don't wish to overhype the comparison—Thomas's film lacks the anachronistic star power of Christopher and Lynda Day George—but there are individual scenes that rival the sheer scale of batshittery that is *Pieces*. And if you're looking to scratch that kind of itch, *Bits and Pieces* is a cheap and fast-healing balm.

Honeymoon Horror

| 1982 | United States | Dir. Harry Preston |

Keystone cops. Everyone's favorite part about the raucous comedy, *The Last House on the Left* (1972).

Literally a schtick as old as film, the concept of the bumbling, incompetent police department was born out of the Keystone cop comedies from the early 1910s. The routine remained a fixture of film for decades, rearing its goshdarn head in things like *Live and Let Die* (1973) and *Smokey and the Bandit* (1977). Entire franchises bloomed from it: *Police Academy* and the French *Le Gardarme* series. Because they are such a cheap and lazy trope, keystone cops met their ultimate destiny within the horror boom of the 70s and 80s. If there were ever an issue with runtime or plot device, a whole host of inexperienced filmmakers put many a husky dude in an ill-fitting uniform to "go check things out."

Such is the case with *Honeymoon Horror*. Directed by Harry Preston, the film is a regional Texas slasher that relies on its keystone cops the same way *Tales from the Crypt* relies on the Crypt Keeper; you don't need him, per se, but the bookends and interludes add an endearing level of spice to the overall experience. Preston, an author of over 90 books (mostly ghostwritten) was a gadfly on the Texas film scene for years before directing his first and only film about a group of young honeymooners being terrorized by a burned-faced freak on a secluded island. Unhappy with the final product, producer and financier Michael Wyckoff shot a wraparound story about two dipshit cops who just kinda exist in the background, hilariously detached from any of the machinations that move the plot.

The movie begins torridly with Elaine (Cheryl Black) cheating with her husband's buddy, Vic (Bob Wagner). After being caught in the act, Elaine kills her hubby by knocking the angry cuckhold unconscious with a beer bottle and letting him fall face-first into the crackling fireplace. Then, following the opening credits, we see a patrol car racing down the highway, lights ablazin'. Are these the first responders to the murder we just witnessed? No, it turns out that an entire year has passed, and the Sheriff and deputy just need some smokes and snacks from the local gas station.

Unimpeded, the story continues with a group of sorority sisters arriving at Lover's Island, a cabin resort now run by Elaine and Vic, newly married. Three of their sisters are honeymooning there the next day, and they want to gussy up their cabins with ribbons, balloons, and messages that say things like "Virgins Need No Urgin." Also, for reasons that go unexplained, Halloween skeletons. One by one, the three women are offed by an ax-wielding madman, but since Elaine assumes they left the island once finished, no suspicions are aroused.

As worried parents are wont to do, they call the police to report the girls missing. However, the Sheriff, parked and relaxing near a lake, is furious to hear this come across the radio (radio being a regular telephone inside his car). He berates his deputy, insisting he wait longer before investigating, then unbuckles his pants and wades out shin-deep into the lake, standing in serene meditation.

If you've seen *The Burning* (1981)—or any movie ever made—you know who the killer is and how this all unfolds, so I won't waste time rehashing it here. But I will say: don't believe the negative hype written about *Honeymoon Horror*. Though clumsy as hell, the film is a lively and entertaining gem lost to VHS purgatory. Nowhere else will one find such choice dialogue:

"Something just touched me!"

"Maybe it was the bridge?"

But before we go, we must check in on the Sheriff, who is dawdling about town following the horrific events of the film. A car pulls up, a pair of newlyweds looking for directions to Lover's Island. The officer of the peace loses his shit and fires his pistol into the air, screaming. The married couple drives away in terror. End credits.

Gutterballs

| 2008 | United States | Dir. Ryan Nicholson |

The world lost a good one in 2019, when filmmaker and special effects artist Ryan Nicholson succumbed to brain cancer. Hailing from British Columbia, Nicholson provided makeup and special effects work on television shows such as *The X-Files* and *The Outer Limits*, as well as the films *Blade: Trinity* (2004) and *The Chronicles of Riddick* (2004). But more important to our endeavor here, he was an artist who never skimped on his vision, whether the constraints were budget, talent, or good taste. And though he directed a handful of extreme horror films under his Plotdigger Films banner, none will live forever in infamy like *Gutterballs*.

Imagine if the films from the Video Nasties era actually lived up to the hysteria, and you're beginning to understand the madness that is Nicholson's second feature as director. Imagine, again, all those times a buddy said, "check this out, it's really fucked up," and you do, only to be let down by the hype. Well, *Gutterballs* is satisfyingly fucked up. Some much so, an English Protestant mom from the 80s will materialize out of nowhere to finger scold you: if you watch this film, you'll go to prison! And if you're in prison now, it's probably because you watched *Gutterballs*!

Breaking the film down to its most basic elements, *Gutterballs* is a love letter to 80s slashers and the rape revenge exploitation films of the 70s. No time period itself is defined or called out, but the characters don the Decadent Decade's garish garb, yet bowl in a modern bowling alley. The nonsensical rivalry that drives the story reeks of "Beat It," while the sardonicism reaches for *South Park*-level crassness.

Just as inscrutable, too, is the movie's tone. For a majority of *Gutterballs'* runtime, the hijinks land somewhere north of Troma and south of Ruggero Deodato. Extremely vulgar, politically incorrect, and heightened to cartoonish levels, Nicholson aims for laughs—albeit for one, obvious instance: a real-time, vicious gang rape scene.

To get there, we begin with two rival groups bowling against each other. It's never explained why people who utterly despise one another spend so much time bowling together. But alas, they bowl, and following a series of physical altercations, the janitor (Dan Ellis) boots them…for the night. They're free to come back tomorrow to finish their game. Because, why not? One doesn't start a game of bowling with one's nemesis and not finish. This isn't Afghanistan.

One of the women, Lisa (Candace Lewald), forgets her purse and sneaks back inside the bowling alley to retrieve it. She is then ambushed by the group led by Steve (Alastair Gamble), a preppy douchebag who's as misogynistic as he is vile. They pin Lisa to a pool table and take turns violently assaulting her, in what must be the most reprehensible rape scene I've ever seen. The film is only 96 minutes long, and it feels like the assault lasts for 95 of those minutes.

Fortunately, it ends, and we settle back into the obscene—and rape-free—groove established prior. The next night of bowling arrives, and with it, an upside-down-bowling-bag-masked killer waiting to strike (heh). It's clear to the audience that the slaughter is revenge for Lisa, but the movie keeps everything a hush-hush-whodunnit until the very end. This uncertainty doesn't impede our ghoulish enjoyment when the slashing starts, however. There are many creative ways to kill someone in a bowling alley, and nobody deserves such creativity more than these shithead characters.

Hilariously enough, the signature kill of the film has nothing to do with bowling, insofar that the bathroom floor of a bowling alley is a natural place for couples to 69. That's right. Hormones get the better of two characters, who find the quiet solitude of the dirty restroom floor to, uh, swap ends. Which is convenient for BBK (Bowling Bag Killer), as he(?) smothers and suffocates each lover on their respective privates.

Death by 69, baby.

Gutterballs is nasty and mean and sets new standards for depravity. If *Cannibal Holocaust* (1980) and *The House on the Edge of the Park* (1980) are too Sunday school for you, this is your next step up. Just be sure to wash your brain with hot bowling ball wax once you're finished.

The Majorettes

| 1986 | United States | Dir. S. William Hinzman |

The Majorettes is technically a slasher movie, in that a psycho killer is picking off members of a high school majorettes team one by one. However, by the end of the second act, the film has gone so far off the rails, someone might walk in and assume you're watching a cheap *Rambo* knockoff. Which sucks, because now you must restart the movie to prove to this dingus that they're only half right.

But it's not all suckage. The opening credits are five minutes of pure sleaze; the majorettes dance for the yearbook photographer as if Larry Flynt has a gun to their head. Each majorette dances their own (erotic) solo, while yearbook dude is on his knees, twisting and turning, and snapping pictures like some pervy dirtbag. Then we meet the wacky stock characters:

- A star quarterback who's sad because the town "dope pusher" knocked up his friend on the majorettes team
- The "dope pusher" himself, a villainous, low-level, suburban criminal named Mace Jackson
- An evil German nurse, Helga, who with her mentally challenged son, plots to kill her elderly charge for the inheritance
- The "big time county" homicide detective called in to investigate by the religious nut local sheriff
- And for small portions of the film, majorettes

For its first third, *The Majorettes* is your standard substandard mid-80s slasher, but as mentioned above, there's a significant shift in tone and genre after the midway point. A lazy writer would call it a move toward crime and action. An intelligent writer wouldn't be writing this at all. And me, an ambitious dumbass, I call it Bonkers Ass Cinema.

For example, members of Mace's gang appear as if each was pulled separately from *West Side Story, Cruising,* and *Deliverance.* One is even wearing neo-confederate garb—in Pennsylvania? He also carries an old timey pistol from the Civil War, because it shoots musket balls and thereby can't be traced by the police. (I guess they wouldn't look for the only guy in town with the gun that shoots musket balls.)

S. William Hinzman, the director, needs no introduction to horror fans, as he plays the cemetery zombie in the beginning of George Romero's *Night of the Living Dead* (1968). Similar to Romero's early films, *The Majorettes* is extremely low budget and shot in the Pittsburgh suburbs. It's also written by *Night of the Living Dead* scribe John Russo, adapting it from his novel. (Note to self: acquire this novel.)

Like Vaseline on toast, the overall experience is one of taking a mundane, weird recipe and adding the funniest shit from your medicine cabinet. Classification and edibility questions may arise, but it's nothing compared to the ease in which it mashes against your gums. Mmm.

The Zodiac Killer

| 1971 | United States | Dir. Tom Hanson |

Say what you will about any other aspect of 1971's *The Zodiac Killer*, but the film itself is the first of its kind—and to my knowledge, the only one ever made—whose *raison d'être* was to catch an active serial killer.

The eponymous serial killer in question terrorized the Northern California region in the late 1960s with seven confirmed victims (two of which survived) and became a media sensation when he began taunting the police with phone calls and sending cryptic letters to journalists (where he claimed to have killed 37 people). David Fincher's *Zodiac* (2007) is the definitive retelling of this story, but that film doesn't hold a candle to *The Zodiac Killer*'s off-the-wall goofiness and shear ambition of purpose.

Enter: Tom Hanson.

Hanson was, for lack of a better expression, a rather shady businessman, who owned a bunch of Pizza Man franchise stores in Southern California. In the early 1970s, his modest business empire began to crumble, and he owed money to people all over town. On the documentary made for the AGFA Blu-ray release, he said about the situation: "If I'm going down, I think I'll knock out a picture or two on the way down—which I did."

Indeed, he did. According to Hanson on the commentary track, he wasn't interested in film at all and didn't even like it. It was purely a business venture with one objective: gain as much notoriety as possible (and in return, profitable returns) by making an exploitation movie that would catch the Zodiac killer; the guiding principle behind the idea being that the Zodiac Killer had such an inflated ego that he couldn't resist showing up to the San Francisco premiere.

Thus, *The Zodiac Killer* was made cheaply and quickly in an effort to get the movie out while the killer was still active in the Bay Area. On a budget of $13,000, Hanson and crew worked fast to accumulate 90 minutes of usable film by setting up in various L.A. locations without permits, shooting one take, and heading to the next location.

You can probably guess this sort of amateurish, guerilla-style filmmaking didn't lead to impressive results. And you'd be slightly wrong. Sure, there's terrible acting, atrocious dialogue, and no coverage shots whatsoever. But surprisingly enough, Hanson had some innate technical craft when it came to shooting and editing together the murder and action sequences. If you've seen Fincher's *Zodiac*, the haunting Lake Berryessa

The Zodiac leaves his mark at Lake Berryessa. Photo courtesy of the American Genre Film Archive.

murder scene most likely sticks with you to this day. It's one of the most effective scenes ever filmed. However, I think the same scene portrayed in Hanson's film is equally effective and creepy. Not to mention, you get the hilarious line from the killer: "I'm gonna have to stab you people."

The actual structure of the film is also equally stupid and creative. The first half hour serves as a fun, little exercise in misdirection as we follow two suspicious gentlemen around San Francisco in their daily lives—the point clearly being that one of them is the Zodiac Killer. Scenes oscillate between a misogynist, insecure truck driver and a misogynist, down-on-his-luck mailman (with an even more misogynist neighbor) who tells caged bunny rabbits in his basement, "If people were as good natured as you, we wouldn't have any trouble in this world."

Wanna take a guess who the killer is? And did the overarching masterplan work? Did Tom Hanson catch the Zodiac Killer?

Well, no, but it wasn't for lack of trying. He did hold his premiere in San Francisco, where he somehow got Kawasaki to donate a motorcycle for him to raffle off. To win, each ticketholder filled out a raffle card that said "I think the Zodiac kills because… ." Lo and behold, they had someone inside the raffle box examining each card to see if any of the handwriting matched the letters sent to the *San Francisco Chronicle*. If this person found something of significance, he was to push a button to alert the people that were… well, outside the box.

All for naught. Bupkis. But the film kicks ass.

Fatal Games
| 1984 | United States | Dir. Michael Elliot |

Sometimes one simply requires a soiree within the comforting, life-sustaining bosom of a cheesy 80s slasher. The nurturing nudity. Brain-cleansing dialogue. Goopy gore. And a whodunnit that lingers in your consciousness for years, because if they're *who*, am I *I*?

For these times, escape into the bosom of *Fatal Game*'s endless bosoms. A slasher still confined to the analog prison of VHS, the film follows on the heels of the genre's golden period (1980-1983) like a lint brush for your dog, picking up tropes and story tics without any regard to their individual and contextual elements. Imagine rebuilding your dog from scratch with its hair and dandruff, and you are beginning to understand the magical pastiche of *Fatal Games*.

Also known as *The Killing Touch*, *Olympic Nightmare*, and (my personal favorite) *Killerspiele*, Michael Elliot's film concerns the goings-on at the Falcon Academy of Athletes. There, young co-eds train for the Olympics by taking steroids, withstanding sexual advances from their coaches, and even learning a thing or two about love. Oh, and dodging the unlimited supply of javelins thrown by a hooded serial killer with no compunction for the glory of USA gold.

Fatal Games feels dated by 1984 standards, but oddly prescient for the decade that would follow; i.e., it plays out like a live action R.L. Stine or Christopher Pike novel, while the killer has a similar vibe and aesthetic to the killers of the late 90s slashers. But more importantly, the film's dated and been-there-done-that quality is its biggest selling point for fans of the genre. *Chicken Soup for the Slasher Enthusiast's Soul*.

Blood Beat

| 1983 | United States, France | Dir. Fabrice-Ange Zaphiratos |

The regional slasher. The Christmas slasher. The ghost samurai slasher. The regional, Christmas, ghost samurai slasher.

Blood Beat ticks those boxes—not with a pen dutifully scratching through prompts on a page, but with a pipe bomb. When someone says "regional, Christmas, ghost samurai slasher," you feel like you've seen it a thousand times. Yet, this American-French co-production blows these conventions sky-high until they rain down like smoldering and delicious cheese curds, reminiscent of the film's idyllic, Wisconsin setting.

Directed by Frenchman Fabrice-Ange Zaphiratos, *Blood Beat* stars Claudia Peyton as Sarah, a woman coming home to her boyfriend's mother's rural Wisconsin home for Christmas. Cathy, the mother (Helen Benton), senses right away something amiss with Sarah and tells her son, Ted (James Fitzgibbons), that she's had visions of Sarah before. Ted shrugs it off; that's just mom being batshit crazy again!

Sarah then finds a trunk in her bedroom with old samurai getup, which might have something to do with a ghost samurai covered in blue light going around the neighborhood, slaughtering hapless Wisconsinites. As the film unfolds, there appears to be a kind of symbiotic relationship between the samurai's power and Sarah orgasming all over the place. (Yes, you read that correctly.) The film leaves open the question whether or not the orgasm causes the violence or vice versa.

I can tell you want answers, and I don't have them. *Blood Beat* is as impenetrable as it is hypnotic, a film in love with arthouse, slasher, and superhero mythos equally. Whenever someone throws around the term "Lynchian" as shorthand for abstract art, I want to rub my naked body over hatching spider eggs. But in this case, that may be the best descriptor we have. Quality aside, the film is conscious art constructed for the subconscious. Plot takes a backseat to dreamy imagery, while the music pulses and lures one into a coma-like state of mind. It's sexy. It's Americana. It's Lynchian. Just with a ghost samurai.

BONUS INTERVIEW
Todd Ocvirk

Todd Ocvirk is the co-director and co-writer of Kolobos *(1999). A writer of several films, Ocvirk's screenplay* Bashira *was made into a feature film in 2021. This interview has been edited for clarity and brevity.*

Matt Rotman: Regarding *Kolobos*, can you describe to me the main players, how it came to be, and what the process was like?

Todd Ocvirk: Sure, the main players were myself, Daniel Liatowitsch and Nne Ebong. We were all film school classmates at USC. We graduated in 1996. And then a couple years later, we were the first ones out the gate of our class to make a movie. We were in the screenwriting program, which is a small class. So first, Nne and Dan started kicking around ideas for making a movie. And then they asked me to join them, which I was happy to do. We initially started with a script that Daniel had written. It was a completely different story. It was a supernatural kind of psychological story—it was a good script/ But then we decided to do something different instead, and that ended up being *Kolobos*. And so our investor we got through Nne; her mom at the time was the accountant of Ed [Taylor].

Ed gave us the money and just gave us free reign to make what we wanted. And so we did. The script started off very differently than how it ended up. I think the film was ahead of its time in some ways. After it came out, and I saw another film do something similar, I certainly didn't think they ripped us off by any means, or anything like that. But you can kind of see some elements of *Saw* in *Kolobos*.

And our first draft of the script, it was a lot like *Saw*. The characters would have to solve these puzzles in order to escape. And if they didn't solve the puzzle, then they would get killed. And everything was being filmed; the villains at the time were crazed film school students trying to do a reality show type of thing. It was a lot more elaborate and, unfortunately, required a bigger budget than we had. So we had to basically scrap all of that and made this more psychological, weird, Italian *giallo* throwback instead.

MR: Yeah, I was going to ask, how did the Italian stuff get in there? That's one of my favorite parts of the movie.

TO: Yeah, absolutely. Daniel, he's from Switzerland. I'm from Hawaii. And we grew up watching the same kinds of horror films. European horror was big at the time. We quickly bonded over those movies, and they came into play with *Kolobos*. That's where the Italian influence came from.

At the time, *Scream* was really big, and there were a lot of *Scream* type movies, *I Know What You Did Last Summer*, *Urban Legend*, that kind of stuff. We wanted to do something that was a bit more geared toward hardcore horror fans, so we did something that had a little of the *Scream* elements, but was clearly influenced by Italian horror.

MR: When you say you were ahead of your time, that's another aspect I think of, too. Definitely with the *Saw* stuff, as we went through ten years of torture porn right after your film. But then there was another ten years of retro throwbacks. Everything is throwback now. It seems you were unfortunately the first one out the gate, and it may have hurt you a little bit. But I also think that's why people are catching on now.

TO: I appreciate that. But yes, a little bit ahead of our time. Unfortunately, we kind of missed the boat on some stuff, and maybe if we had a bigger budget with better production value, it could've gotten seen a bit more at the time. But I don't want to say it got lost in the shuffle of direct-to-video horror in that era, because it did okay. It did okay when it came out. I was just happy to get a movie made.

MR: One of the things I picked up on in the film, subtextually, is the theme of what is real? What is reality? Does it matter? And it's all wrapped around a reality TV angle. Was that conscious when you guys were making it?

TO: Yes. When we decided to take this new approach to the movie, we definitely went for more of a psychological angle. For sure. Films like *Repulsion* was another influence.

MR: I didn't even think about that, but yeah, that makes a lot of sense.

TO: We took that, and we ran with it. At the time, *The Real World* had just come out. And it was Daniel who really came up with that concept. I wasn't really into that show, because the characters were annoying. I think that was probably the point of the show. But he just one day said, "Man, what if there was a show where these people all got killed?" And that was basically the seed of *Kolobos*.

MR: Your characters in the movie are perfectly annoying.

TO: Yes, they are. On purpose.

MR: So we all know—that you know that I know the [*Kolobos*] theme song is *Suspiria*.

TO: [Laughs] Yes, it is. It's a quote unquote homage.

MR: Who wrote that? I assume it was obviously on purpose.

TO: Absolutely. Our composer was a guy named William Kid. Great guy. Loved that guy. I was actually his assistant at USC. He was a film composer, so when I had the opportunity to do this film, he was the first person that I thought of, just because I knew him. And he happily agreed to help me out. We put together a pretty good temp track that had a lot of Italian music, Goblin music, cues from *The Shining*. Due to the budget and time constraints, we basically told Bill, "Just make it like this." To which he added his flair. But certainly the theme is a riff on *Suspiria*. No doubt about that. Some people bash it because it copies it, but other people love it, because it's an homage to that theme. So however you want to take it, it was clearly influenced by *Suspiria*, and I can't hide that.

MR: My only critique is that I wish it was used more in the movie. It's only at the beginning and end.

TO: Yeah, it was a great theme. He did a great job. I got to sit in on some of the sessions he did with the vocalist. He did such a wonderful job with the little he had to work with.

Monsters

7

THERE ARE MONSTER KIDS and everyone else. The kids who collect every variation of the Wolf Man mask and the kids on the school bus who pour soda on them. Children who beg their mom and dad for a subscription to *Fangoria* or *Famous Monsters* and the ones imploring their parents to watch *Charlie Rose*. Because they're sickos.

I first saw *Creepshow* (1982) when I was six or seven and instantly became a Monster Kid. "The Crate" scared the ever-living shit out of me, sparking a lifelong obsession with monsters, horror, and the addict-like urge to feel that original sensation of absolute terror. (Fellow horror fiends have appropriately dubbed this pursuit "chasing the dragon.")

To boot, when my parents divorced, I found myself stuck for hours on end in my dad's shitty, Divorced Guy apartment. The internet didn't exist then, so if you didn't want to read books about war, you had the TV and an endless supply of VHS bootlegs. It was there I became best friends with Godzilla and King Kong, Frankenstein and the Wolf Man. I watched the skeleton army in *Jason and the Argonauts* (1963) on repeat.

And I use the word "friends" with great purpose. As trite as it is to say, the childhood love of monsters is empathy for the outsider. Dracula is a guy who wants to love. Frankenstein was given consciousness and life by Man and shunned as a freak. Godzilla was born from a fireball of nuclear energy and attacked simply for existing. The Invisible Man, well, he's just a prick.

The Monster Kid—the loner kid—relates to all of this. However, it's more. Coming of age with the classical monsters is coming of age with the most *personable* monsters. The Jack Pierce Wolf Man makeup. Teizō

Toshimitsu and Akira Watanabe's Godzilla design and Kanji Yagi's suit. These creatures feel alive and full of personality. Their anguish is your anguish. They are as real as your real-life friends.

Obviously, in this chapter, we are going well beyond the classical monsters of yesteryear. But that love, that personal connection to the freak, that kinship to these creatures which began in my dad's apartment thirty years ago—that will be our anchor as we float out into the void of the wackiest monster films known to man.

The Milpitas Monster

| 1976 | United States | Dir. Robert L. Burrill |

My favorite aspect of *The Milpitas Monster* isn't its wholesome, Americana charm. Nor is it the film's endearing behind-the-scenes story of an entire city coming together to help a teacher and a group of students make a Z-grade monster movie. No, my favorite part is that despite all that—a community pulling resources to accomplish a common goal—they would end up creating a film that makes their community look like complete and utter shit.

Indeed, the ambition, scope, and full-scale local support needed to accommodate the former two are the stuff Feel Good Vibes are made of. Director Robert L. Burrill, a photography teacher at the high school in Milpitas, CA, spent three years turning his short film about a monster created from the town's pollution into a feature length picture. With the city's explicit backing, they gave Burrill full access to the municipality's firetrucks, police cars, and helicopters. Local businesses even chipped in, paying $50 to have their names listed in the film credits. Therefore, the $5,000 film feels *massive*.

Massively stinky.

That's because in order to have a monster born of pollution, one must have pollution. And ideally, lots of it. I have no idea if pollution was a big concern for the citizens of Milpitas in the 70s, but Burrill spends so much time showing us how fucking disgusting the city is. The overflowing landfill. Streets and yards strewn with trash and shit. Garbage floating in waterways. Hell, our avatar into the story is a homeless drunk who wanders through the city, experiencing the monster at seemingly every turn.

Milpitas underwent such an effort to make their city appear so unpleasant, but I'm glad they did, as we got a fun, weird ass regional film out of it.

Of course, *The Milpitas Monster* suffers from the same things all regional cheapies do: friends and non-actors performing at their sublevel-community-theater best, amateur editing and sound design, and more filler than ice in a McDonald's soda. All that's to be expected. What one does not expect to find in films such as these is a rather cool, retro monster design.

A mix between Mothra and Mothman, the monster of Milpitas comes to life through a combination of stop motion and guy-in-a-suit practical effects. Its eyes glow eerily and shots from the creature's POV see a world of glistening prisms like that of a fly. Cloth, unmovable wings hang rigid on its back to complete the perfect formula of 1950s science fiction cheese. However, unlike many works from that era, a sense of personality shines through, similar to the best Toho monster films.

The plot—hilariously—resolves around the monster, pissed about the buildup of trash in Milpitas, stealing folks' trashcans, which becomes a citywide outrage. Political intrigue ensues: "More missing garbage cans, mayor. Isn't anyone looking into the matter?" Riots and protests break out. "WE WANT OUR GARBAGE CANS" read the protestors' signs.

And just as the City of Milpitas joined together to make *The Milpitas Monster*, they, too, must rally their forces to defeat it.

Death Bed: The Bed That Eats

| 1977 | United States | Dir. George Barry |

Sometimes the monster is under your bed. Other times the monster is the bed itself.

Such is the case with George Barry's delirious 1977 film, a work made particularly infamous by Patton Oswalt's standup bit:

> This guy wrote *Death Bed: The Bed That Eat People* [sic], took it to a second guy and said, 'Okay, it's called *Death Bed: The Bed That Eats People*. Now the backstory is, there's a demon—' And the second guy says, 'stop drilling, you hit oil!'

The gist of the entire routine is how intimidating it is writing screenplays for major studios when guys like George Barry just make movies about killer beds without all the political hassle. Now, Barry might take issue with a number of items from the bit, most specifically with how universally

The bed that loves to eat... hand skin. Photo courtesy of George Barry and Cult Epics.

famous Oswalt is compared to himself. Secondly—and intentionally or not—the comedian's premise completely undermines how fucking hard it was for Barry to make *Death Bed* and sell it. With no budget, he spent five years piecemealing the film together just for every distributor to say no. That alone is an insane feat, considering everything that was distributed between 1970 and 1979.

Death Bed: That Bed That Eats lives now as a staple of ironic viewing for many a hipster, a cretinous cohort we choose not to associate with, given our Bonkers Ass Ethos. And certainly, due to the amateur nature of the production, there's a lot to poke fun at. But that neophyte veneer hides a truly unique art film that anticipates you laughing at it and gets in on the joke. For such a dark fairy tale, the movie is littered with wacky, self-aware moments, such as when the bed has an upset tummy and chugs a bottle of Pepto Bismol. Which, to me, negates whatever motivation one might have for ironic viewing.

The film is a series of stories or vignettes of characters coming into contact with the titular bed and being eaten. A voiceover narration stitches everything together, coming from one of the bed's victims who is trapped inside a painting and must witness each murderous act. Through the narration, we learn how the bed came to be: a demon once fell in love with an earth girl, so he turned himself into human form to sleep with her. Unfortunately, he was too powerful and killed her in the act of lovemaking, for which he cried tears of blood onto their bed, giving it life.

And, boy, that demon bed sure is hungry. It eats apples, buckets of fried chicken, champagne, flowers, jewelry, and entire orgies! Once a person or item is ingested, Barry films them floating in a yellow liquid substance, shots that have an uncanny semblance to the Piss Christ.

Because there's no true narrative arc to the story, the overall pacing feels a bit wonky, and you can sense the protracted production. However, with a hilariously high body count and hypnotic score, it's never boring. (The gore gags and short running time help, too.) But the real draw is Barry's fascination with the imagery and commitment to art design over plot. He doesn't give a shit how or why these characters came to be in contact with the bed, but he sure likes killing them in style.

Project Metalbeast

| 1995 | United States | Dir. Alessandro De Gaetano |

You gotta believe me. I've looked. *Project Metalbeast* is not a Full Moon production. I've scoured IMDBPro, gone down the Wikipedia rabbit hole, and even checked under my bed—including lifting up the skinfolds of my wife's secret, naked lover to see what's under him. Nada. Zilch.

Which is odd, because *Project Metalbeast* has all the hallmarks of a Full Moon film: a cheap 90s aesthetic, character actors from the 70s on their second wind, and a great hook squandered on a small budget and middling production. This is neither an indictment of the movie nor Full Moon, simply a casual observation we all know to be true, if we're honest with ourselves. In fact, *Project Metalbeast* succeeds for the same reason the best Full Moon movies do. It's bad-fucking-ass.

The film, directed by Alessandro De Gaetano (*Bloodbath in Psycho Town*), tells you everything you need to know upfront, written out right there on your screen:

> **Operation: Lycanthropus**
> **Objective: Sample werewolf blood**
> **Purpose: Create superior combat agent**

These words precede a secret military operation where Donald Butler (John Marzilli) and another soldier sneak into a foggy, very Hammer-looking castle estate. Butler has no problem sacrificing the other dude to an attacking werewolf, shooting it with silver bullets as it munches down on dude's neck. Extracting the beast's blood, Butler takes the sample back to his boss, Colonel Peter Alexander Miller—played by none other than Barry Bostwick.

Unfortunately for the operation, the stupid scientists use up most of the blood studying it, forcing Butler to inject the remaining tidbits into himself and making him a werewolf for endless study. A team player he may be, a werewolf is still a werewolf, and Butler ends up murdering one of the scientists before Colonel Miller can kill him with silver bullets and cryogenically freeze his body.

Fast forward twenty years, the body is still sitting on ice when scientists figure out a way to replace human skin with a prosthetic material made of metal alloy. Well, sort of. They can't quite seem to get it to work. But Barry Bostwick has an idea! How about using the technique on werewolf skin?

The Colonel gives the brainiacs Butler's body to play with, and during the operation, they discover the three silver bullets in his chest and remove them—for which you can probably guess what happens next. We now have a live werewolf with indestructible metal skin! *Oops*.

You'll notice that I have given a much longer plot synopsis than I usually do, and that's because there's a lot of plot to this fucking thing! *Project Metalbeast* feels more like the condensed first season of a television show than a standard three-act film, up to and including the boring midseason doldrums. Thankfully, the movie has a fantastic beginning and end, bookends to cleanse the aftertaste of a very plodding middle.

What the film gives you instead of wall-to-wall action is a fantastic creature design. The werewolves at the start look like cheap *Bad Moon* (1996) prototypes with a dexterous range of facial expressions, while the Metalbeast design at the end is a true, intimidating sight to behold. The suit is made for the bulky behemoth of Jason Vorhees himself, Kane Hodder, who utilizes the same aggressive posture he pioneered in the later *Friday the 13th* chapters.

But yeah, yeah, yeah. It's a freakin' metal werewolf. Check it out!

Blood Freak

| 1972 | United States | Dir. Brad Grinter |

Blood Freak opens with director Brad Grinter seated and smoking a cigarette. Glancing down every three to five seconds to read from the script, he speaks into the camera with that double-edged, apathetic sternness of a post-War dad:

> We live in a world subject to constant change. Every second of every minute of every hour—changes take place. These changes are perhaps invisible to us, because our level of awareness is limited. Take for example, the things we do and say to the people we meet. All these things affect our lives, influence our destiny, and yet there seems to be some kind of fantastic order to the whole thing. We never know how or when we will meet a person who will become a catalyst—or who will lead us to one. What is a catalyst? Well, in this case, a catalyst is a person who will bring about change. They could be good or bad, but there will be changes. You can meet one almost anywhere in your everyday life. In a supermarket, drugstore, anywhere. Even riding down the Florida Turnpike. A pretty girl with a problem. Who could resist? Certainly not Herschell.

First off, I'm sure a lot of destinies have been irrevocably altered driving down the Florida Turnpike (Aileen Wuornos comes to mind). Secondly: doesn't that monologue sound, you know, kinda stoner-dorm-room-talky for one of the most infamous anti-drug films ever made?

(Side note: my wife is currently looking over my shoulder, rolling her eyes at the *Blood Freak* poster. Eventually, she says, "but hey, at least that girl has a nice rack." Now, I roll *my* eyes: "Of course she has a nice rack, it's a Christian film.")

And *oooh boy*, a Christian film, indeed. As a matter of fact, *Blood Freak* may be the pinnacle of 1970s Christian anti-drug turkey-man monster exploitation. The other films in the genre just can't touch it. Okay, well, you got me. There aren't any other films. But the Judeo-Christian literary tradition of CRAZY-ASS, HYPERBOLIC ALLEGORY is as old and robust as Man Itself.

I'm thinking, of course, of Jonah and the Whale.

Naturally, a modern thinker and rhetorician may overlook this story and others of its ilk (David and Goliath, etc.), surmising that the introduction of the *fantastique* ironically dilutes the message and power of God, since the heightened aspects of the story don't mirror reality and thus erode the possibility of a supernatural, all-powerful being. And don't worry, if you're not following me, it's only because you don't have *Blood Freak* brain.

The point is, if you wanted to convince a godless philistine to believe in God, wouldn't you tone it down some? Why do missionaries always start at 11? Maybe begin with: hey, if you go to church every other sabbath, it'll make your psoriasis slightly less worse. Or, look at this fucking sweet tax write-off! Salvation also comes with a 20% coupon from Buffalo Wild Wings ($50 minimum purchase).

But back to Jonah. The main thrust of it is this: God was totally bragging to Jonah that he was gonna Sodomize the city of Nineveh, but he totally wouldn't if Jonah went to tell them he totally would. God is basically Anthony Fauci at the beginning of the pandemic when it comes to whether you should wear the mask—masks do help in preventing the transmission of the virus, but you shouldn't be wearing one… [wink]. What the fuck?

Yet Jonah, that rascal, fled from his duty (and ultimately, God), and thinking he was just hired as a staff writer for the second season of *Fear the Walking Dead*, decided to escape his problems via boat. And we all know how that ended. A storm hits, God saves Jonah (but fuck all those other Jews on the boat who did nothing wrong) by having a whale swallow him. Jonah, seeing the true mercy of God, repents, and the whale pukes him up, so he can go show Nineveh all that sweet whale goo.

Jonah defied the commands of God and strayed in sin, but upon seeing God's true power and forgiveness, returned to the heavenly fold. Which is the exact same story structure as *Blood Freak*. Minus a blood freak or two.

The Herschell introduced in the opening monologue is a wandering, aimless Vietnam vet cruising around on his motorcycle when he picks up this smoking hot Jesus freak, Angel (see what they did there?). Doing what any good missionary would do, she takes him to a raging drug party, where she instructs him adamantly: no drugs. No, the zonked-out writers of the Gnostic texts would never want that. There, while everyone else is having fun, Angel sits Herschell down and sermonizes endlessly about how God hates anything cool.

Being a Good Samaritan, Angel brings Herschell home to stay with her family. He immediately meets her father, who offers him a job at his poultry farm. In the meantime, Herschell encounters Angel's sexually liberated younger sister, Anne while cleaning the pool (they really put his ass to work). She coerces him into a little pot and sex, and thus, the age-old story of weed addiction begins.

Herschell begins his employment at the family farm in between shifts smoking weed like a crack fiend. Taking advantage of the situation, two scientists performing experiments on turkeys bribe Herschell with grass to be their Guinea pig, in which he has to eat their tainted poultry to see if there are any ill side effects. You can probably guess where this is going.

Never take a toker to a turkey farm, as my dad used to say.

One night, after some bad bird, Herschell has a seizure and loses consciousness. Apparently not bound by any FDA regulations, the two scientists find his body and toss it into the woods, assuming he's dead. Herschell wakes up, transformed into the hideous Blood Freak: all man, except for a giant turkey head. Much like Cain, he wanders the land in shame, slaughtering and eating drug addicts (complete with hilarious ADR'ed turkey gobbles littering the soundtrack).

Now, I don't want to give away the horribly contrived ending, but let's just say Herschell has a chance to complete his Jonah-esque arc, correct the errors of his ways, and redeem himself in the eyes of the Lord.

A lot of folks—even loving fans—rag on this film as Ed Wood-level amateurishness, and I honestly couldn't disagree more. Sure, the acting is rough. Steve Hawkes is the biggest name here, and he was only minutely known at the time for playing Tarzan in a series of Spanish films. Every other actor is what you might expect to find in this type of affair. So not great.

But there is a strange level of craft going on that you don't normally see in an Ed Wood or Herschell Gordon Lewis film: i.e., Brad Grinter actually shoots some coverage! There are closeups and genuine edits between characters talking. The pacing holds together better than a thousand similar films. There's a reason why *Blood Freak* has clung to the cult world the way it has all these years.

And much of that is due to the movie's earnestness. Grinter set out to make an evangelical film that could play in grindhouses and drive-ins, but he didn't make a Christian exploitation film, he made an exploitation Christian film. It's just as much a love letter to the blood and sex of the genre as it is a sincere message film (the name Herschell is an obvious nod). At the very least, he didn't feel the more exploitative elements were beneath him, something many genre directors are often guilty of.

If the road to Hell is paved with the best of intentions, *Blood Freak* may quite well be the inverse.

Attack of the Beast Creatures
| 1985 | United States | Dir. Michael Stanley |

Filmed in Connecticut, *Attack of the Beast Creatures* takes on the defining quality of its locale, in that the film, much like the state, is more important for what it's close to than what it actually is. Whereas the character of Connecticut comes from its proximity to New York City, the charm of Michael Stanley's film is that in 1985, it had more kinship with a 60s Roger Corman or Eddie Romero exploitation yarn than the types of horror films being released the same decade.

The movie is goofy and gory, quaint and crudely rendered. It's the type of film where actors hold wooden dolls to themselves and shriek in agony. Where three-quarters of the budget is spent on a face melting scene and characters say stuff like, "we need to build a shelter to protect us from those things!" *Those things*, of course, being cheap, hand-controlled puppets that attack our cast with abandon.

And for some reason, it's a period piece. "Somewhere on the North Atlantic, 1920" the films begins, as a group of passengers float aboard a life raft, the only survivors of a devastating shipwreck. They land on a deserted island, and in search of food and water, they discover a tribe of creatures, who are literally animated Zuni dolls (think *Trilogy of Terror* [1975] and you'll know exactly what I mean). The creatures, delighted by the unexpected food source, descend on the survivors by the dozens, biting and clawing. A repetitive massacre, one after another.

Attack of the Beast Creatures is a backyard film—no doubt about that—but it elicits the same joy one gets from watching better films explore Skull Island or the giant, exotic creatures of *Mysterious Island* (1961). A project of pure passion, this movie will remind you why you like genre cinema in the first place.

○ ○ ○

DIRECTOR SPOTLIGHT:
Eddie Romero

Without a doubt, the upper echelon of the cinephile community is riddled with secret handshakes, gatekeeping tics, and enough hipster energy to power a turntable in a blackout. Indeed, one of the lofty, naïve goals of writing this book was removing such pretensions and barriers from the conversation, so we can celebrate cinema together. There is no test at the end of this. No forbidden knowledge or passwords. Yet, if our paths ever do cross, there is one quick way into my heart, a shibboleth phrase to instantly bypass my introverted defenses: "Eddie Romero."

Utter that to me and all of a sudden Fiona Apple's "excruciating" night with Quentin Tarantino and Paul Thomas Anderson, all coked up and talking about film, will seem like an NPR roundtable. You will try to politely nod and excuse yourself, but I will forcefully grab your wrist and insist, "but I haven't even gotten to the Fifties yet!"

Not to overhype, but there should be a giant, Leninesque statue of Romero greeting you as you sail into Manila Bay. In the American embassy, where the photo of the U.S. president sits next to the Filipino president, there needs to be a third photo of—

—okay, you get the point.

In the parlance of *The Big Lebowski*, Eddie Romero was "the man for his time and place." His rise in the Filipino film industry coincided directly with America's insatiable appetite for drive-in fodder, and his collaborations with Kane W. Lynn at Hemisphere Pictures and Roger Corman at New World Pictures jumpstarted an entire cycle of exploitation films shot and set in the Philippines. If you like Pam Grier and those Jack Hill women-in-prison films, *The Big Doll House* (1971) and *The Big Bird Cage* (1972), pour one out for Eddie.

Terror Is a Man

| 1959 | Philippines, United States | Dir. Gerardo de Leon |

Romero began his creative career at age twelve, publishing short stories and working as a journalist for his father's newspaper. Director Gerardo (Gerry) de Leon approached Romero in the early 1940s—when he was just sixteen—soliciting the young writer for screenplay help. Romero went on to write several Filipino films prior to the Japanese occupation of World War II, before directing his first film, *Ang Kamay ng Diyos* in 1947. Throughout the 40s and 50s, he wrote and directed movies that spanned all genres: war and political films, comedies and dramas. But it was his co-production with de Leon and Kane W. Lynn in 1959 that completely altered the Filipino industry landscape.

Terror Is a Man is a classical monster movie made for the drive-in market, and it succeeds wildly, despite its scattershot identity. In fact, the film, directed by de Leon, is as good as any of the Universal entries that inspired it. A mad scientist. A sympathetic monster. A little romance. What more do you need?

Well, how about an expressionistic, noir visual palette, a touching, humanistic script by Romero, and a creature design that rivals the best of Jack Pierce's work? Toss in some gore, and that filly in the back of your pop's Studebaker will need to be pried off you with the Jaws of Life. (Early on in what would become a pattern of showmanship and marketing for Lynn, a narration card was placed at the beginning of the film to warn sensitive viewers that a bell would sound before the oo-ey, goo-ey stuff, so they had time to turn away.)

The plot also sets the pattern for a lot of the Hemisphere horror films that followed: i.e., your main character(s) show up on an isolated South Pacific island, and there's a mad doctor doing shit. In this case, the unfortunate outsider is William Fitzgerald (Richard Derr), an American sailor and sole survivor of a shipwreck. William is found washed ashore by Dr. Charles Girard, played by the great Czech actor, Francis Lederer. The doctor, as he explains to William, moved to the island with his wife (Greta Thyssen) to do his experiments in peace, away from the moral, prying eyes of society. And, oh yeah, a boat only comes every few months, so make yourself at home!

What follows next is an exercise in horror and moral relativism, half inspired by *Frankenstein* and half by the experiments of Josef Mengele. As mad scientists are wont to do, Dr. Gerard couches his inhumanity in

Poster for *Terror Is a Man*. Photo courtesy and copyright Independent-International Pictures Corp.

scientific objectiveness as he pursues the next level of human evolution, merging animals and humans together, without any regard or sympathy for his test subjects. Where later Romero films would portray the mad scientist as a flamboyant Doctor Moreau-type character, Lederer leans hard into the dark European ethos that dominated the prior decade, creating a sinister and formidable adversary for William to overcome.

Terror Is a Man was a minor hit, but its importance to the Filipino film industry cannot be overstated. For one, it introduced horror to the country as a profitable genre. And two, perhaps most importantly for exploitation film buffs, the Hemisphere Pictures partnership between Romero and Lynn bridged the film economies of America and the Philippines. In the same way Americans invaded Canada during the Tax Shelter Era, ambitious go-getters like Roger Corman saw Filipino co-productions as a viable way to sustain their cheap, run n' gun exploitation business model.

Mad Doctor of Blood Island

| 1969 | Philippines, United States | Dir. Eddie Romero, Gerardo de Leon |

Now, Dear Reader, before we continue, I must insist we all take the Oath of Green Blood. Repeat after me:

> I, a living, breathing creature of the cosmic reality, am ready to enter the realm of those chosen to be allowed to drink of the Mystic Emerald fluids herein offered. I join the Order of Green Blood with an open mind and through this liquid's powers am now prepared to safely view the unnatural green-blooded ones without fear of contamination.

And thus begins *Mad Doctor of Blood Island*—with another one of Lynn's wildly unusual promotional gimmicks. A prologue introduces the film inviting all patrons to recite the Oath of Green Blood and drink some "green blood" distributed by the theater. The oath was written by legendary producer and distributor Samuel M. Sherman, who worked for Lynn at the time.

The film itself is the third entry of Hemisphere's "Blood Island" series, which started with *Terror Is a Man* and *Brides of Blood* (1968). The latter film is of particular note, because it began a years-long collaboration between Romero and star John Ashley. Ashley went on to star in many of Romero's films, but he also took on a producer role, even starting his own company, Four Associates Ltd, to help fund their ventures.

Spanish poster for *Brides of Blood*. Photo courtesy and copyright Independent-International Pictures Corp.

In *Mad Doctor of Blood Island*, Ashely stars as Dr. Bill Foster, one of the poor saps arriving on Blood Island in the film's setup. Foster is a pathologist sent to investigate a strange disease that turns people into green-blooded lunatics. He is joined by Sheila Willard (Angelique Pettyjohn), who is trying to reconnect with her alcoholic father and Carlos Lopez (Ronaldo Valdez), who is trying to get his mom off the island. The titular mad doctor is Dr. Lorca (Ronald Remy), a fearful island presence that is somewhere between Doctor Moreau and a proto-Jim Jones (nice sunglasses!).

Romero co-directs with de Leon, and together their style is considerably more standard exploitation than the film noir tones and shadows that dominated *Terror Is a Man*. However, they employ one of the most unusual camera techniques I've ever seen, in that every time the monster is in a scene, the zoom focus quickly goes in and out on repeat. This creates a sense of dislocation and immediacy, which is oddly tactile. Obnoxious, sure. But once you get used to it, you feel uncomfortably in the middle of the terror—arguably the primary purpose of any horror film.

Beast of the Yellow Night

| 1971 | Philippines, United States | Dir. Eddie Romero |

The real selling point of *Mad Doctor of Blood Island* is Romero's script. His characters and their arcs are as fully formed as you're going to find in an exploitation film. He has no problem slowing the proceedings to a complete halt to let you into Carlos' tragic family drama, which seems boring at the time, but by the end, pays off in spades. The exact same can be said for *Beast of the Yellow Night*.

Romero, Ashley, and Lynn finished off the "Blood Island" series in 1970 with *Beast of Blood*, the biggest seller of all the "Blood Island" movies. Immediately afterwards, Ashley put up the funding for the next film through Four Associates Ltd and cut Lynn and Hemisphere Pictures out of the deal, instead opting to go with Roger Corman's virgin New World Pictures for distribution. The film, *Beast of the Yellow Night*, remains as odd today as when it was released—an intellectually-minded exploitation feature that doesn't seem at all concerned with delivering "the goods," insomuch as with the moral struggles of its characters.

Ashley plays Joseph Langdon, an American army deserter turned criminal in Southeast Asia. A murderer, rapist, and thief, he avoids death and the immediate fires of Hell by striking a deal with Satan (Vic Diaz). The deal is that Langdon must inhabit the bodies of others and bring out the latent evil of all those around. Everything is going smoothly until Satan has Langdon come back as Philip Rogers—with Langdon's original face. Philip's wife, Julia (Mary Wilcox) seems to have no qualms with her husband looking like someone else and takes this opportunity to fix their marriage.

During this period, Langdon fixates on the concept of salvation and ponders with increasing dread the ramifications of his deal. Satan—aware of his shifting loyalties—makes it so whenever Langdon tries to exert free will and repress his innate evilness, he becomes a murderous werewolf. Which, taken in the larger pantheon of werewolf mythos, I can get behind.

First of all, I am always a sucker for Man Rebelling Against His Own Fate stories. Combine that with a werewolf film, and you have my full attention. Generally speaking, the werewolf metaphor tends to lean one of three ways: puberty, repressed sexuality, or the feminine cycle. In *Beast of the Yellow Night*, Romero uses the concept as man turning against his inner self and his true inner self manifesting into reality—cutting out the middle man of metaphor altogether. Original Sin isn't an abstract thing, but a known quality that you can see... and can kill you.

Romero's genius is that once the cerebral becomes tactile, the focus is squarely on character. And, luckily, Ashley is up to the task of giving us that extra layer needed to pull this off. When the final gut punch of the climax hits you, you'll realize you were always in the hands of two artists who knew exactly what they were doing.

Twilight People

| 1972 | Philippines, United States | Dir. Eddie Romero |

Along with *Beast of the Yellow Night*, Corman hit paydirt with a slew of women-in-prison films in 1971 and 1972, most notably the Jack Hill movies mentioned previously. (Romero would even go on to direct one of the more popular entries of the genre, *Black Mama, White Mama* in 1973). But perhaps the biggest winner of this film cycle was Pam Grier.

Before her first starring role in *Black Mama, White Mama*, Grier had memorable side gigs in the first wave of women-in-prison films, as well as Romero's *Twilight People*, where she played Ayesa the Panther Woman. Like *Island of Lost Souls* (1932), I don't know what it is about casting really hot women as Panther Women, but consider me Panther Woman-curious.

Actually, *Island of Lost Souls*—a riff on H.G. Wells' *The Island of Doctor Moreau*—is the pretext for *Twilight People*. All of the "Blood Island" films that came before had the Doctor Moreau story on their minds, but this is

Romero's most literal interpretation. Well, literal in the only way Romero knows how.

The Edward Prendrick character from the novel, a learned Englishman who survives a shipwreck, is replaced here with Matt Farrell (John Ashley), an American mercenary. Farrell is kidnapped while scuba diving and brought to the island of Dr. Gordon (Charles Macaulay), who is trying to create the ultimate human specimen out of man and animals. There's the previously alluded to Panther Woman, Kuzma the Antelope Man, Primo the Ape Man, Lupa the Wolf Woman, and Darmo the Bat Man. Farrell is next on the list of surgeries, but he and Gordon's daughter (Pat Woodell) escape the compound with the test subjects and must survive in the tropical jungles, being pursued by Gordon's team of hunters.

I won't beat around the bush here: *Twilight People* is an insane picture, the epitome of New World Bonkers Assness. Yet, there is a goofiness that's endearing and an electric guitar soundtrack that gives it a nice, modern sheen. The weird, homoerotic chemistry between Ashley and his pursuer, Steinman (Jan Merlin) is also an interesting touch and probably way more on the page than it was intended to be. Out of all of Romero's films, *Twilight People* is the one I've seen the most, and the one I'd most likely screen for newbies—after they've said "Eddie Romero" to me in public and wake up on my couch with a chloroform hangover.

○ ○ ○

The Being

| 1983 | United States | Dir. Jackie Kong |

There are filmmakers who cannot help but speak the language of cinema. Natural filmic storytellers born with some innate skill, or who simply soaked in thousands of hours of film, to the point of completely rewiring their brains. Scorsese is such a filmmaker. As are Wilder, Spielberg, and Tarantino.

Toss Jackie Kong into that category, too.

Married to Smut Master General William Osco, Kong had zero filmmaking experience when her husband handed her a few million to make a movie in 1980. Osco, known primarily for producing the porn parody, *Flesh Gordon* (1974), had zero acting experience when he decided to star in said movie (under the hilarious pseudonym, Rexx Coltrane). Yet, despite the obvious handicaps, Kong fashioned a ridiculously watchable film and one of the best monster movies of the 80s.

The Being begins with a *Twilight Zone*-esque voiceover introducing you to the quaint, rural town of Pottsville, Idaho. Everything is perfect there—if you discount all the citizens who have gone missing. Detective Mortimer Lutz (Osco) is on the case and soon lands hot on the trail of a monster, a mutation caused by a local nuclear dumping site.

Similar to *Jaws* (1975), Kong maximizes the limitations of her production by showing very little of the creature for much of the film. In fact, the copious use of a prop monster hand—like the function of the shark's fin in Spielberg's film—is almost all we see until the final act. Kong fills the interim with relentless humor and kinetic, fast-paced editing. It also doesn't hurt to have Martin Landau in a small role as a chemist who covers for Big Business. (Yes, dumping nuclear waste into your drinking water is completely safe!)

For whatever reason, *The Being* catches flack for being a so-called *Alien* rip-off. If you hear or read this opinion, write it off immediately. There must've been some International Convention of Hipsters a while back that landed on this theory, probably because the monster has a phallic-like head. That's literally the only connection. Kong's film has more in common with films like *The Thing from Another World* (1951) and *The Blob* (1958) than *Alien*. Unless, of course, I've been watching Ridley Scott's film wrong all these years, and it's really just a funny, 1950s monster movie throwback. Ridley, you wacky dude, you!

The Monster of Camp Sunshine

| 1964 | United States | Dir. Ferenc Leroget |

This film could have easily been in the Sexploitation chapter. *And why wasn't it*, you ask. Well, to be perfectly honest, I had not yet seen *The Monster of Camp Sunshine* when I was writing that section of the book. *This is 2022. Couldn't you just go back and insert the film in your Microsoft Word document*, you ask again, really starting to bug me. Yeah, but it's called **The Monster** *of Camp Sunshine*. Maybe if it were *The Boobies of Camp Sunshine*, I would take a class at the local community college, actually learn how to use a computer, and then go back and fix it.

I stand behind my decision, if only because Ferenc Leroget's one and only film lacks genre classification altogether. Half nudie-cutie, half nudist camp film, half silent film, half surrealist comedy, and half horror movie, *The Monster of Camp Sunshine* wears many hats while the characters wear little else. As if a warning for the anachronistic shenanigans to follow, the film opens with a series of title cards, reminiscent of the silent era:

"The motion picture that follows is a fable.... .

In it there are many nudes but only one monster.... .

In life it is generally the other way around."

Then, a title card with the alternate title: *The Monster of Camp Sunshine or How I Learned to Stop Worrying and Love Nature*. Ah, yes. A not-so-subtle poke that we are entering very heightened territory—perhaps even on the level of a great Peter Sellers romp.

Don't get your hopes up.

That being said, get them a little up. While not in the same ballpark as *Dr. Strangelove*, the movie is legitimately funny. Funny, too, in a slightly more sophisticated way than most nudie-cuties, which traditionally aim

The monster of Camp Sunshine. Photo courtesy of the American Genre Film Archive.

for low-brow slapstick and juvenile wordplay. And if you can stick it out to the end, your reward will be a massive, Bonkers Ass sequence most big budget comedies don't dare attempt.

Unfortunately, in order to get there, you must traverse the typical slog inherent to these types of films. As such, the plot is meaningless and discussion of it even more so. Women go to a nudist camp. Women are attacked by a local man gone crazy after ingesting weird chemicals. That's literally it.

The camera hangs still scene after scene as ladies undress and walk around, all kinetic energy dying in a pool of antiquated sleaze. However, in the same way you expect a gun fight every ten minutes in a spaghetti western, *The Monster of Camp Sunshine* throws bizarre, comedic jabs in almost systematic intervals—punches to the brain groin, making sure you're still awake. A lab rat throwing a nurse out of window? A five-minute sequence of a guy fishing and only catching trash?

More of a curioso for the hardened Something Weird fan, the film still offers wacky pleasures for the patiently willed.

Invasion of the Aluminum People
| 1981 | United States | Dir. David Boone |

While not one to traditionally review short film—*Invasion of the Aluminum People* clocks in at an efficient 29 minutes—I'm also not above making the occasional exception. Especially when a film is exceptional in every conceivable manner.

The plot of *Invasion of the Aluminum People* is best described by way of quantum mechanics, in that for every particle, there is an opposite antiparticle (for example, for every electron that exists, so does a positively charged positron). Antiparticles make up antimatter, whose relationship with regular matter composes our observable reality with non-observable offshoots (alternate dimensions). Therefore, using quantum mechanics, we could legitimately theorize that when *Invasion of the Aluminum People* was made in the Dallas, TX of our observable universe, endless other variations were made in the countless, *more weird* Dallases of the multiverse.

Statistically speaking, then, a "normal" version of the film exists. And in this "normal" version, the plot is thus: a secret government organization discovers a race of aluminum people who subsequently take over the

Nothing like a little outdoor telly. Photo courtesy of Louis Black Productions.

world and reshape society. One member of the organization, *Invasion of the Body Snatchers* style, rebels against the inevitable change and runs until he can run no more.

All of this happens in the version we know (I think?), but there is nothing linear or concrete to draw coherent conclusions from. Images accompany a soundtrack out of control with collages, ADR dialogue, and a futuristic score. Characters with no introduction pop in and out and say odd things like: "We don't have time for sex-hurt! We've got to call the Army, the Navy, the Air Force!"

The film is art house, no bones about it. Yet, it adheres to the genre-adjacent realm much like its brethren, *Tetsuo: The Iron Man* (1989) and *Eraserhead* (1977). Whereas the latter two films play footsie with horror, David Boone's short tangos with 1950s science fiction, and its black and white photography recalls Ed Wood just as much as the onscreen pageantry oozes early MTV.

Invasion of the Aluminum People is weird and dense and generally indescribable. But with such a short running time, it remains relatively palatable, even to the most semi-curious.

Rock 'n' Roll Nightmare

| 1987 | Canada | Dir. John Fasano |

If there's ever been anything in the universe that willed itself into existence from nothingness, out of the ether, into the unbearable lightness of being, it's Jon-Mikl Thor. Sure, that could probably be said of most Canadian pseudo-celebrities, but Jon-Mikl is a special case.

Born into a working class immigrant family from Vancouver, John Mikl always wanted to be a superhero. He wore a Superman costume under his school clothes and had kids throw bricks at his head to prove his invincibility. Inspired by the likes of Steve Reeves, he entered his first physique championship as a body builder at age 14, later becoming the first Canadian to win both, Mr. Canada and Mr. USA.

Chasing stardom, he moved to Hawaii in the 70s to take part in the live nudie show, *What Do You Say to a Naked Waiter?* and quickly transitioned into music thereafter. Mikl was deeply influenced by the theatricality of bands such as KISS, Alice Cooper, and Bowie and, thus, branded himself Thor. The newly minted alter ego utilized his ripped bod, elaborate costuming, and fearless showmanship to score an RCA record deal and brief stint as a British metal sensation.

Unfortunately, Jon-Mikl Thor would never be Mr. Universe or have a hit single in the United States. But that never stopped him or slowed him down. Rising from the ashes of nothing to be the most mediocre something in everything, film acting was, of course, the next, logical step.

Enter: *Rock 'n' Roll Nightmare*. With a childhood love of monster B-movies and superheroes, Thor penned a script for a horror film that combined the two passions. He drew from his experiences as a semi-successful musician and set up what's essentially a haunted house story around a rock band attempting to record their next album at an abandoned farm. Thor stars as a version of himself, a buff as hell front man, who—with his band mates and their girlfriends—confronts an ancient evil that begins offing them one by one.

Sounds routine, right? And it kinda is, if you ignore the parade of batshittery that inhabits each scene.

After a rather boss righteous cold open, where a malevolent force sucks a housewife into the oven and cooks her, we go into an eennnndddllleeesss credit sequence. You know, the kind of credit sequence that has a different title card for each person and role? And after the oh-God-did-I-forget-to-walk-the-dog-and-give-Mom-her-pills-and-I-should-really-get-checked-for-ADHD credit sequence, we finally fade into the establishing wide with the band's tour van driving along the desolate Canadian roads to the isolated house. And then we continue with establishing wide shots of the band's tour van driving along the desolate Canadian roads to the isolated house.

I have clocked this sequence. From the fade-in to the van arriving at the house: three minutes and forty-six seconds! Mind you, the credits are over with! We're just watching the van drive for four minutes. It's *The Deer Hunter* wedding scene of van driving.

But I assure you, if you just power onward, the van does arrive. For which then we're treated to the best on-screen defense of the Canadian tax shelter ever. When a bandmate asks Thor why they've traveled all the way to Canada to record the album, he responds: "Because Toronto is where it's happenin', man. The music, the industry… the arts!"

You sold me.

You might intuit from my snarky tone that I don't like this movie. And you'd be right. I fucking *love* this movie. What the film sacrifices in competence, it makes up for in pure heart. I mean, who doesn't love the *Evil Dead II* ripoff shot, where the camera flies throughout the house, then up the stairs—but halfway up, sorta slows down as if the cameraman got winded? That's filmmaking heart, my friend.

(I haven't even gotten to the extended shower sex scene with Thor and his girlfriend—a Melvin van Peebles in *Sweet Sweetback's Baadasssss Song*-level of sleaziness where the star is just using the film to get some. You just gotta take my word for this one: it'll give you some much-needed confidence in your French-kissing game.)

My favorite element, though, is the film's reliance on practical makeup and creature effects. Yeah, it ain't the end-all-be-all use of latex masks, and the creature puppets are more Jim Henson on ketamine than *Alien*, but it works, somehow. Everything in the end adds up to a charming, yet goofy lo-fi 80's sensibility. And if you don't like that, why are you even reading this?

Ninja Zombie
| 1992 | United States | Dir. Mark Bessenger |

Landing somewhere between Troma, Cannon, and *Deadbeat by Dawn* (1992), Mark Bessenger's film is at once all those things and a singular entity that exists in its own universe and plays by its own rules. The very type of movie that motivated me to write this book.

Ninja Zombie, shot entirely on Super 8 in Chicago, was conceived by one hundred nine-year-olds at one hundred typewriters and written in five minutes. Containing zombies, ninjas, voodoo, and occult artifacts, the 1992 film cultivates every pulp staple, tosses them into a martini shaker, and pours 100-proof shots of childhood imagination. Indeed, to connect these two metaphors, the experience of watching the film is like hanging out with a drunk nine-year-old.

The eponymous ninja zombie is Jack Chase (John Beaton Hill), a smitten karate expert who begins the movie proposing to his girlfriend,

Just because you're dead doesn't mean you can't dress like a badass.
Photo courtesy of the American Genre Film Archive.

Maggie (Kelly Anchors). Unfortunately for him, his best friend, Orlan Sands (Michael Correll) shows up, asking Jack for help. Orlan is being hounded by Spithrachne (Terry Dunn), leader of the Red Spider Cult, who exudes the exact same scenery-munching energy as Treat Williams in *The Phantom* (1996).

As Orlan is filling Jack in on the deets, one of Spithrachne's goons appears and murders Jack following the film's first fight scene. Orlan, desperate for a bodyguard, tracks down voodoo practitioner and tennis player, Brother Banjo (Michael Weaver), a jovial fellow with no compunction assisting Orlan raise Jack from the dead. Now a golem-like husk of a man (sporting a black vest and no shirt), Jack must regain his karate skills and take down the Red Spider Cult before they get their hands on a mysterious artifact that can do… *something*.

The ambition of *Ninja Zombie* is breathtaking. Despite the micro budget, Bessenger crafts a globe-sprawling film full of wonder, magic, and lots of ninja action. In fact, you could pair this perfectly with John Carpenter's *Big Trouble in Little China* (1986) and not lose a beat. So don't let the kitschy title steer you away from this one. It's a total knockout.

Bigfoot 8

THINK OF THIS CHAPTER as a brief addendum to Monsters. A deranged primate postscript, if you will. Instead of *Sophie's Choice*-ing a whole host of great Bigfoot films in the last chapter, I decided to just include a short walkthrough of the wackiest Sasquatch entries here.

Which is no easy task, as the Bigfoot genre lends its Ass to the Bonkers. For whatever reason, few filmmakers can simply create a straightforward, A-to-B Bigfoot movie. I don't know why, but there's something about depicting the legendary ape man on celluloid that brings out the inner weird of all who try. Bad for the Positive Bigfoot Representation Community, perhaps, but great for us.

That being said, there are two elements of a Bigfoot film that pop up again and again. One is the depiction of the creature as a slasher killer. While this element is typically treated like a stalk-and-slash animals attack film, there are many instances of Bigfoot utilizing tools and weapons (axes, knives, sticks, etc.), similar to a standard slasher. Either way, the creature is almost always shown as a murderous and hostile force.

The other feature of the genre that rears its head like clockwork is Bigfoot needing to kidnap human women for breeding purposes. You will see in this chapter that this Weird Ass idea appears as early 1970's *Bigfoot*. It's probably best to check in with a social psychologist to explain this particular phenomenon, but since I got you by the ear, I may as well give you my theory: hairy backs.

The 1970s was the pinnacle age for the hairy back. When your dad got up from the recliner after finishing his TV dinner, the chair's fabric was just ripped to shreds by his course-as-fuck, manly-as-shit back hair. The sexiest man in America had a fro sprouting out the back of his shirt to the bottom of his neck, like a Disco Stu cancerous growth. If you didn't smell like talcum powder, full-flavored beer, and back hair dandruff, they kicked you out of grade school.

Naturally, Freud explains the rest. You can't have all these sexy, back-haired dads around the house without daughters getting a little subconscious crush. Therefore, an entire generation of women came of age sexually attracted to hairy beasts. But things were about to change.

As women fought for empowerment in the 60s and 70s, their desire for hairy backs waned. Instead, they wanted more: groomed and sculpted men—guys who had the audacity to take care of themselves. Which created a societal predicament. We now had a generation of young girls attracted to hairy backs and a bunch of older men with hairy backs who couldn't get women. So we invented the Bigfoot film.

I hope that's clear.

Shriek of the Mutilated

| 1974 | United States | Dir. Michael Findlay |

Michael Findlay and his wife, Roberta made a name for themselves in the short-lived "roughie" cycle of the 1960s, pushing the limits of sex and sadomasochism in a genre known for pushing the limits of sex and sadomasochism (*Body of a Female*, *The Touch of Her Flesh*). Then, in 1976—without any foreknowledge—the couple traded in their notoriety for even more notoriety with *Snuff*, a re-edited version of their shelved 1971 film, *The Slaughter*. It turns out, producer Allan Shackleton secretly filmed a new ending that purported to show a real-life murder on-screen and released it under the guise of that gimmick.

In between these two career phases came *Shriek of the Mutilated*, the setup of which is standard for any Bigfoot film: a college professor takes his students into the woods to find undeniable proof the Yeti exists. However, once we're in the woods, nothing is standard or routine. At least in the way words mean anything at all.

A quick pre-credit sequence kicks things off in a cool, proto-slasher fashion, with a woman being decapitated by an axe-wielding...

sasquatch? Cut to Professor Ernst Prell (Alan Brock) lecturing four of his graduate students about the Yeti and their upcoming journey to find it. Afterwards, the students cut loose at a very seventies-rific party, where they encounter Spencer St. Clair, the sole survivor of Dr. Prell's last Yeti-scouting trip seven years ago. He's now an alcoholic and suffers from PTSD, raving about being attacked by the creature and narrowly escaping.

A great bit of exposition, if it ends there, right? *Oh, no.* We follow Spencer home where he completely melts down and slits his wife's throat with an electric carving knife. Okay, awesome, even if it stops there. *Nope.* Immediately after, Spencer is sitting fully clothed in the bathtub, drinking a beer, and half-assedly scrubbing blood from his shirt. Unbeknownst to him, his wife has survived the ordeal. She grabs a toaster, crawls bloodily through the house to the bathroom, plugs in the toaster, and tosses it into the bathtub, killing Spencer. Okay, *surely*, it ends there! It actually does. But in another version of this film, I could totally see these two trying to one up one another *Spy vs. Spy* style into perpetuity.

The next day, Prell and crew begin their trip into the wilderness. There, they encounter what is probably my favorite use of the clichéd-old-man-harbinger-warning-of-doom character ever. When one of the students asks the old man if there's something they should beware of, he responds: "It might not make much sense to you, but it makes sense to me."

But yeah, okay, I lied. We're not going into the woods. We're going to some guy, Karl's house, where the rest of the movie takes place. Karl is a professor buddy of Prell's, who claims to have heard the Yeti in the forest surrounding his home. From here, the group will search for the Yeti—and it's also from here I won't give anything else away. There is an insane plot detour that is not to be spoiled, though you might be able to sus it out halfway through.

My favorite aspect of *Shriek of the Mutilated* is that it turns into a type of "creeping dread" movie, à la *Let's Scare Jessica to Death* (1971) or *Kill List* (2011). A kind of slow-burning mystery (unbearably slow at times) where a bigger conspiracy against the characters is unveiled. The last fifteen minutes are fantastic and don't even feel in the same universe as to what came before. Very fun, very pulpy stuff.

Terror in the Swamp

| 1985 | United States | Dir. Joe Catalanato |

"You two numbskulls take your boat and go up Bluebird Bayou. I'm going up the Hooch. We'll meet at Alligator Point."

That's the kind of local flavor you soak up in the regional monster film, *Terror in the Swamp*. Shot on the cheap in the swamps of Houma, Louisiana, the movie is sweaty and wet and chockfull of thick, Cajun accents—some so impenetrable they had to be redubbed by different actors.

And I say "monster film" in lieu of "Bigfoot film" purposefully. Sure, the creature looks like a Bigfoot, acts like a Bigfoot, and lives in a region known for its Bigfoot lore and films (see 1976's *Creature from Black Lake*, for example). But it's really a giant, mutated nutria with manlike features that are never convincingly explained.

The film, directed by first-timer, Joe Catalanato, is even structured like a Bigfoot slasher, or at least for the initial half. Taking a cue directly from *Friday the 13th* (1980), the stalking sequences are all shot from Bigf—I mean, the Nutriaman's POV, as if Mrs. Voorhees herself is traipsing through the murky, moss-littered water. These shots glide gracefully across the swampy marshland like on a floating Steadicam track, though they were most likely achieved by placing the camera on the front of a fan boat and slowing down the footage in post. It's a nice little touch that adds tremendous production value to such a small film.

Plot-wise, *Terror in the Swamp* is two films: the first half, which plays like a slasher or animals attacks movie, and the second half, which is essentially *It's a Mad, Mad, Mad, Mad World* (1963), only with a Nutriaman instead of cash. Following the grisly attacks that begin the film, the race is on to capture the creature, as the game warden, local sheriff's department, drunken hunters, redneck poachers, military commandos, and mad scientists descend into the swamp, shooting each other by accident and getting blown up with rocket launchers. Complete pandemonium, I tell you!

Originally distributed on VHS by New World Video, the film has since fallen out of print (as of this writing). Which is a total shame, too, because with the cheap-looking VHS and bootleg DVD covers of a Bigfoot-like creature looking in through a set of windows, one would never assume this was anything more than a standard, schlocky Bigfoot movie—when, in fact, it's something much bigger. And weirder.

Bigfoot's Bride

| 2021 | United States | Dir. Erick Wofford |

There are a litany of standard mistakes unseasoned filmmakers commit. (Trust me, I know.) Whether it's careless sound design, fucking up simple match edits, or trying to do much with the budget, the list isn't unique to any green director. Some learn. Others wash out pretty quickly.

Exceptions prove the rule, as they say, and Erick Wofford's first feature, *Bigfoot's Bride*, is the proverbial odd man out. Microbudget to the core, the film is a fully realized vision completed with the technical skill needed to overcome the limitation of resources. The sound is full, and the color design is purposeful. Remarkable attention is paid to the creature design, while the gore is particularly inspired; the practical effects are augmented with cartoon blood splatter, an obvious penny-pinching move that feels like a deliberate, creative decision the longer the movie plays.

Bigfoot's Bride is also profoundly weird.

If you can somehow imagine the perfect amalgamation of *Bride of Frankenstein* (1935), *Cannibal Holocaust* (1980), and *Night of the Demon* (1980), you'll be somewhere in the ballpark of what this film offers. Bigfoot—nicknamed "Fred" in the credits because he wears a mechanic's uniform with that name, presumably stolen from one of his victims—begins the film doing what Bigfoots do: namely, stalking and slashing all who enter the woods. And after a cold open with a couple hunters biting the dust, *Bigfoot's Bride* slows to a screeching halt, becoming a character piece as we follow the hideous beast around in existential anguish.

Bigfoot is lonely and repulsed by the way he looks, aware of his Otherness the same way Frankenstein's Monster is in the novel and films. At one point, he finds a creepy clown mask in the forest, by which he is immediately fascinated, as he can finally hide his face. Then, right on cue, he is lovestruck by the lovely Heather (Jessica Megan Rivera), a woman coming into the woods to kill herself after being jilted by the longtime boyfriend. The monster can't approach her, of course, so he keeps a distance and observes, even stealing her dirty shorts. In any other movie, this sequence would play extremely pervy, but Wofford shoots Bigfoot not like a voyeur, but like a child full of wonder, experiencing and seeing things for the first time. Whatever sleaze there could have been is desaturated into a moment of sweetness and melancholy.

The unique creature design in Bigfoot's Bride. Photo courtesy of Wild Eye Releasing.

The film takes another one-eighty, a direction I don't want to spoil, but the pacing, atmosphere, and tone remains unabated throughout. Musically, the soundtrack feels like a compromise between faux-M83 and Fabio Frizzi and is the pulsing vessel into the movie's vibrant colors and deliberate pace. A visual and sonic palate that is equal Ruggero Deodato and Spike Jonze.

Honestly, my only critique of the damn thing is that the filmmakers choose to go with the scratchy veneer of a fake exploitation film, including (perhaps anachronistically) pseudo-VHS tracking issues. It's not a dealbreaker in the end, for the budget and arty aesthetic lend room for such a crazy swing, even if it is a little trite in this day and age. Overall, the attention to detail in every other aspect more than makes up for it, putting Erick Wofford on my short list of directors to look out for.

Night of the Demon
| 1980 | United States | Dir. James C. Wasson |

The thin threads tethering you to reality have been severed. Your ego and existential essence are unbound, floating through the ether like a wayward astronaut drifting alone through the cosmos in a spacesuit.

Which can only mean one thing: you just watched 1980's *Night of the Demon*.

For those of you still in good spiritual health, let me explain. This film is about Bill Nugent (Michael Cutt), an anthropology professor, who awakens in a hospital bed horribly injured. The entirety of the film's narrative is a flashback, as he tells his story to the local cops, a tale about taking five of his students out into the wilderness to find Bigfoot. Inside of his flashback, he interrogates Bigfoot witnesses, for which we then enter into secondary flashbacks within the original flashback, thus constructing an intricate and shaky *Inception*-level structure that questions the validity of existence itself. Are you real? Are you really reading this right now, or are you simply inside someone's Bigfoot movie flashback?

I honestly have no idea how to write about this movie. I can tell you it was directed by a guy named James C. Wasson, and that it was on the Video Nasty list in the U.K.. I don't imagine I'll be ruffling any feathers by saying it's an extremely shoddy and inept film with all the usual trappings that entails. But that tells you absolutely nothing about *Night of the Demon*. The only way to understand it is to watch it, to experience every minute detail. To hear dialogue like "Bigfoot's not playing games anymore."

As for me, I began to be allured by this movie's particularly brand of Spanish fly when, very early in the film, Bigfoot awakens a camper in a sleeping bag, picks him up, swings him around in the sleeping thirty times, before tossing him like 20 feet into the brush, impaling him on a stick.

And the movie just kinda continues in this fashion for an hour, essentially a slasher movie where Bigfoot is the killer. The setup for each kill is as follows: the group sets up camp in a different location, then the professor tells a story of someone who was killed by Bigfoot in that very spot (flashback alert!). I don't think anyone dies in real time until an hour into the film.

If *Night of the Demon* is known for anything, it's the scene of an unfortunate biker who pulls over to take a leak, and Bigfoot rips off his dick. Oh, to be a fly on the wall when someone at the British Board of Film Classification saw that! (That scene and the notorious Bigfoot rape scene were both removed from the U.K. releases.)

This film gets my highest recommendation, though just be sure to spin one of those fancy *Inception* tops afterwards.

Bigfoot

| 1970 | United States | Dir. Robert F. Slatzer |

Talk about a movie full of Hollywood royalty. John Carradine. John and Christopher Mitchum. A not-so-subtle parallel to the silver screen monarch himself, King Kong. *Bigfoot* certainly has the pedigree. And it has no qualms trashing it all for the sake of some wholesome, fun Bonkers Assness.

Joi Lansing plays Joi (who else?), a pilot who crashes her small, single-engine plane into the forest outside Red Bluff, California. As she parachutes to safety, we shift gears to Jasper B. Hawks (Carradine) and his cousin, Elmer Briggs (John Mitchum), traveling salesmen making their way through the northern Californian countryside. While attempting a sales pitch at a rural general store, they overhear a biker (Christopher Mitchum) phoning the sheriff that a big creature has kidnapped his girlfriend. The conniving businessman that he is, Hawks offers Rick, the biker, help searching for the missing woman, as he suspects this is the legendary Bigfoot. Capturing one could make them extremely rich, he convinces Briggs.

Thus begins a retelling of *King Kong* (1933) by way of *The Searchers* (1956). Rick's girlfriend, Chris, is brought to a lair and tied to a post next to Joi. They deduce from the small, little freak Bigfoots walking around that they are hybrids, and that these creatures need human women to breed. (This same plot is also used by the insane 2014 film, *Bigfoot Wars*.)

Joi breaks free and is captured by the Big Guy himself and carried away, screaming like a much more—let's say full figured—Fay Wray. Now accompanied by several townsfolk, Hawks, Briggs, and Rick follow in tow, blowing up everything in sight with dynamite. What comes next is straight from the King Kong playbook, albeit with more rapey vibes.

Bigfoot is classic exploitation through and through: bikers, dancing hippies, buxom babes, and a feeling of boredom so profound you might consider seeing what your sock tastes like. But as much as the cheap production tries to suffocate everything, the film's tiny, stupid heart can't help but sneak through. For one, a lot of the movie is shot in Red Bluff, where some of the era's most famous Bigfoot sightings occurred, adding a veneer of authenticity. Second, the entire cast leans hard into the fun—especially Carradine—with no one feeling above the film they're in. Which goes a long way when you're watching someone stuff a pissed off Bigfoot baby into a giant bag.

Demonwarp

| 1988 | United States | Dir. Emmett Alston |

If I have one regret—and I only have one regret—is that I didn't see *Demonwarp* when I was twelve. The film was made squarely for the twelve-year-old brain. In fact, I'm still waiting for some hard evidence it wasn't actually made by twelve-year-olds. If you had asked me what I wanted in a movie at that age, I would have said zombies, aliens, Bigfoot, and boobs. And that's the very essence of *Demonwarp*.

John Carl Buechler, who was decidedly not twelve, wrote the original draft of the screenplay with the intention that he would direct it. Buechler was a special effects guru coming off hot from *Troll, Cellar Dweller*, and *From Beyond*. Apparently, he carried some cachet, as he had Jack Palance attached to *Demonwarp*, until ultimately, Buechler left to direct *Friday the 13th Part VII*, and Palance bailed.

Director Emmet Alston picked up the reigns, and Vidmark (the early iteration of Trimark) had the script reworked to be made on the cheap. They convinced Academy Award winner George Kennedy to come aboard with the stipulation that his daughter, Shannon be given a role. Which in hindsight, has got to be one of the worst deals ever. She's only in the movie for about two minutes before Bigfoot rips her head off. I would say that's a spoiler, but I can guarantee you won't even know which character she is. (I'm guessing this wasn't the star-turning vehicle it was meant to be.)

The movie opens with a UFO crashing through the earth's atmosphere (take your pick whether it's ripping off *The Thing* or *Predator*.) A wandering priest in the 19th century, walking by himself and reciting

Bible passages, witnesses the crash. End of cold open. We cut to Bill Crafton (Kennedy) reconnecting with his daughter (who is, curiously, not played by Kennedy's actual daughter) in an isolated cabin. Their game of Trivial Pursuit is interrupted when Bigfoot breaks down the door, knocks Crafton out, and kidnaps his daughter. End of that cold open.

Now, we're with Jack Bergman (David Michael O'Neill) and a group of friends driving to the same cabin for a weekend of fun… or so it seems. What the group is about to learn is that Jack has tricked them, and they're really there to hunt the Bigfoot that kidnapped his uncle. George Kennedy is also lingering about, camping in the woods, hunting the same Bigfoot.

Without giving too much away, the origin of the Bigfoot creature involves aliens and zombies and stolen radio parts. Oh, just wait until Bigfoot bursts through the door of the cabin, mauls someone to death, and runs away with a ham radio. You'll realize quickly enough that I've spoiled nothing of this film—and that it may be impossible to do so.

I think of Ed Wood a lot when watching *Demonwarp*. Not so much in regard to its dopey amateurishness, but for its pure ambition of scope, coupled with the complete lack of talent to pull it off. There is a certain amount of pleasure in watching someone shoot for the moon, despite their shortcomings in just about every aspect of filmmaking. And that's kind of what I meant by it being a twelve-year-old movie, in that it possesses a high level of imagination in a vacuum devoid of logic, practicality, and cynicism.

Horror Anthologies   9

FOR ME, the anthology format offers the quintessential horror experience, regardless of the individual film or segment. Because when you get down to it, the short story is the traditional vehicle for horror. Of course, horror as a film genre has been around as long as film, but the American horror short story, pioneered by Washington Irving, Edgar Allan Poe, and H.P. Lovecraft, rooted the very foundations of the genre in the American consciousness. The brevity and ability to enjoy in one, brief setting correlated directly to the intimate, oral history of ghost stories, and the basic conciseness eventually lent itself perfectly to the limited space of children's comics in the 1950s (E.C. Comics, etc.).

American (and British) short stories found their way into some of the first horror anthologies made in Europe, like *Unheimliche Geschichten* (Germany, 1919) and *Dead of Night* (United Kingdom, 1945), the latter of which inspired the wave of Amicus anthologies made in the 60s and 70s (*Asylum*, *Tales from the Crypt*, etc.). Roger Corman entered the game with the Poe-influenced *Tales of Terror* in 1962, while Mario Bava delivered the mack daddy of anthologies, *Black Sabbath*, a year later. The 80s were no slouch either, giving us *Creepshow* (1982) and *Twilight Zone: The Movie* (1983), before the 90s popped out the underappreciated classics, *Body Bags* (1993) and *Tales from the Hood* (1995). In our micro attention span culture of today, the format remains immensely popular, as the successes of *Trick 'r Treat* (2009), *V/H/S* (2012), *The ABCs of Death* (2012), and *Southbound* (2015) show.

But I'm guessing you know all this, fellow film geeks. Hence, like the Crypt Keeper himself, let me guide you kiddies through a half century of the anthology underbelly. A journey full of sleaze, "what-the fucks," and unhinged ambition. Stories and segments packed with absolute brain rot—though worry not, there's only a bunch of them.

From a Whisper to a Scream

| 1987 | United States | Dir. Jeff Burr |

Jeff Burr is the Michael Clayton of Hollywood, the unenviable journeyman director studios send in to do the dirty work. They fuck up, he takes the lumps, and they go off into the sunset rich and oblivious, while he descends into disillusionment and despair.

His *Stepfather II* (1989) got messed with by the Weinsteins in post-production. *Leatherface: The Texas Chainsaw Massacre III* (1990) was rat-fucked by the MPAA. *Pumpkinhead II* (1994) was—well, who the hell knows what *Pumpkinhead II*'s problem is.

Yet, before his skin was inevitable hardened by the studio system, Burr was a fresh-faced boy from Georgia who made a movie with his friends. *From a Whisper to a Scream* was a pure passion project, the romantic Hollywood ideal fully realized. A recent graduate from USC's film program and inspired by the bootstrap story of Sam Raimi, Burr and his filmmaking buddies raised enough money to make an entire feature. The result was the All-American Horror Movie, created with the same love and ethos as the original *Evil Dead* (1981).

From a Whisper to a Scream is a great film and a top tier horror anthology. It's also sleazy, icky, and full of enough taboos to make your weird uncle blush. Incest? Check. Aborted fetus monsters? Check. Kids killing adults? I won't stand for that!

And it has Vincent Price and Clu Gulager, to boot.

Price appears in the wraparound as the town historian explaining the evil that has always surrounded the community of Oldfield. His first story, "Stanley," concerns Gulager in the titular role, an awkward-as-hell dude who fucks his sister and has a crush on a sexy coworker. As you might expect, everything ends happily for everyone, and the only irony is how sweet it all is.

Terry Kiser stars in the second story, "On the Run." A criminal double crossed by his girl and associates, Jesse Hardwick (Kiser) is shot and left for dead in a swamp, when he is picked up by hermit, Felder Evans (Harry Caesar) and nursed back to life. Jesse figures out Felder is two hundred years old, using voodoo to stay alive—and not having the best scruples, Jesse tries to take the power of eternal life by force. Again, to happy results.

The lesser of the four stories is "Lovecraft's Traveling Amusements," which is about the doomed romance between a glass eater at a carnival (Ron Brooks) and a local woman (Didi Lanier). While that segment never really takes off, the film turns around quickly with "Four Soldiers," a Civil War set piece that depicts a group of American soldiers who stumble onto a house full of children... of parents they've killed.

In the world of horror anthologies, *From a Whisper to a Scream* stands apart for its high percentage of great segments and rock-solid direction from a first time filmmaker. Unless someone tells you in advance, you would never know this was produced by people who had never made a film before. Confidence and a sense of purpose ooze from every frame. The energy and youth and promise are intoxicating. If you don't want to pick up a camera and shoot your film afterwards, you have no soul.

Necronomicon

| 1993 | United States | Dir. Brian Yuzna, Christophe Gans, Shusuke Kaneko |

Brian Yuzna's interpretations of H.P. Lovecraft have always been more of a thematic riff on the source material than faithful adaptation. *Re-Animator* (1985) and *From Beyond* (1985), both of which Yuzna produced, hold true to the spirit of the author's work, but lack much of the plot the stories are built on. And to be fair, that may be the best approach when tackling Lovecraft.

Mostly because the writer relied heavily on the "indescribable." No joke. Anytime Lovecraft needed to describe something horribly grotesque or terrifying, he literally used the word "indescribable." Before going on to describe it anyway. For instance, in the novella, *At the Mountains of Madness*, he writes:

> It was a terrible, indescribable thing vaster than any subway train—a shapeless congeries of protoplasmic bubbles, faintly self-luminous, and with myriads of temporary eyes forming and unforming as pustules of greenish light all over the tunnel-filling

front that bore down upon us, crushing the frantic penguins and slithering over the glistening floor that it and its kind had swept so evilly free of all litter.

As beautifully as that's written, every person will have a different mental image in their head after reading the same passage. Which is why Yuzna's method is best: take the general idea of the Lovecraft story and commit to a variation on a theme.

Necronomicon is such an exercise. An anthology built around mere pieces of the writer's works, the film delivers the full Lovecraftian experience, while utilizing only a fraction of his ideas, a feat accomplished by making the "indescribable" real. With special effects by Screaming Mad George (*Society*) and John Carl Buechler (*Re-Animator*)—all supervised by Tom Savini nonetheless—*Necronomicon* sidesteps any story miscues by turning the Lovecraftian omissions of gore and creature descriptions into an old fashioned, practical effects showcase.

Yuzna directs the wraparound, titled "The Library," in which H.P. Lovecraft himself (Jeffrey Combs) visits the library of a secret order of monks to find the legendary Necronomicon. The book is then used as a vehicle to tell the other three segments: "The Drowned" (based on "The Rats in the Wall"), "The Cold" (based on "Cool Air"), and "Whispers" (based on *The Whisperer in Darkness*). As mentioned previously, "based on" is doing some heavy lifting here; the correlating source material really just serves as the kernel or seed for each concept.

Christophe Gans (*Brotherhood of the Wolf*) steps in to direct "The Drowned," the best of the three and the one with the most Lovecraftian flavor. Edward De Lapoer (Bruce Payne) inherits a seaside mansion in New England. Using the Necronomicon, De Lapoer brings his dead wife back to life—and buyer beware! Mixing the classic "the dead should remain dead" trope with an impressive Cthulhu-like monster, "The Drowned" is a top tier Lovecraft reimagining.

Narratively, the film loses some steam after such a high point, though it never dies completely. Directed by Shusuke Kaneko (*Gamera: Guardian of the Universe*), "The Cold" holds strong up until the ill-advised shock ending destroys all the good will built up by the rest of the segment. The story centers around a young woman (Bess Meyer) and her relationship to a mad scientist (David Warner), who needs a constant cold temperature to stay alive. But it turns out cold ass dudes get all the chicks, and a love triangles threatens to turn up the temperature.

The last story, "Whispers," directed by Yuzna, is a misfire in every way but the special effects department. Beginning *in media res*, two cops chase a fleeing suspect in their cruiser. At the wheel is Sarah (Signy Coleman), who is putting her partner, Paul (Obba Babatundé) back in the Friend Zone after he knocked her up. While arguing, they crash and encounter two bumbling aliens that rock their world with barbarism and ancient rites. Unfortunately, the humor Yuzna goes for doesn't land, but it doesn't matter. The creature design and gore effects steal the show with hideous bat demons and gratuitous limb amputations.

In fact, the mood, creature design, and freewheeling sense of fun really carry the entire film all the way through. A true gem lost to the VHS era (as of this writing), Necronomicon deserves a high definition restoration—if only to fully appreciate the special effects mastery on display.

Macabre Pair of Shorts

| 1996 | United States | Dir. Scott Mabbutt |

Talk about a film with peaks and valleys. *Macabre Pair of Shorts*, a Troma Team release, is certainly on brand with its lo-fi presentation and big dream aspirations. However, inspiration alone cannot paper over the lack of execution to keep the horror comedy firing on all cylinders. The result is a fairly plodding, middle of the road anthology with interesting ideas and no payoffs—except for two, remarkably unique segments, both of which deserve mention here.

The wraparound framing is Joe Dante's *Matinee* (1993) by way of *Clerks* (1994). Two loser employees at Panavision find an old film can with a reel entitled *Macabre Pair of Shorts*, so they spend their Halloween screening it in the company's private theater. *Macabre Pair of Shorts*, as it turns out, is a horror anthology itself with each segment a television program watched by two vampires.

Which brings us to "The Legend of Seymour Hackell," the second of the stories (the first, "MPS," about two women vampires encountering some hijinks with a would-be victim, is strangely underwritten and not worth going into detail over). This second entry, inspired by Washington Irving's "The Legend of Sleepy Hollow," turns the film around immediately by delivering the endearing, low-budget oafishness Troma is known for.

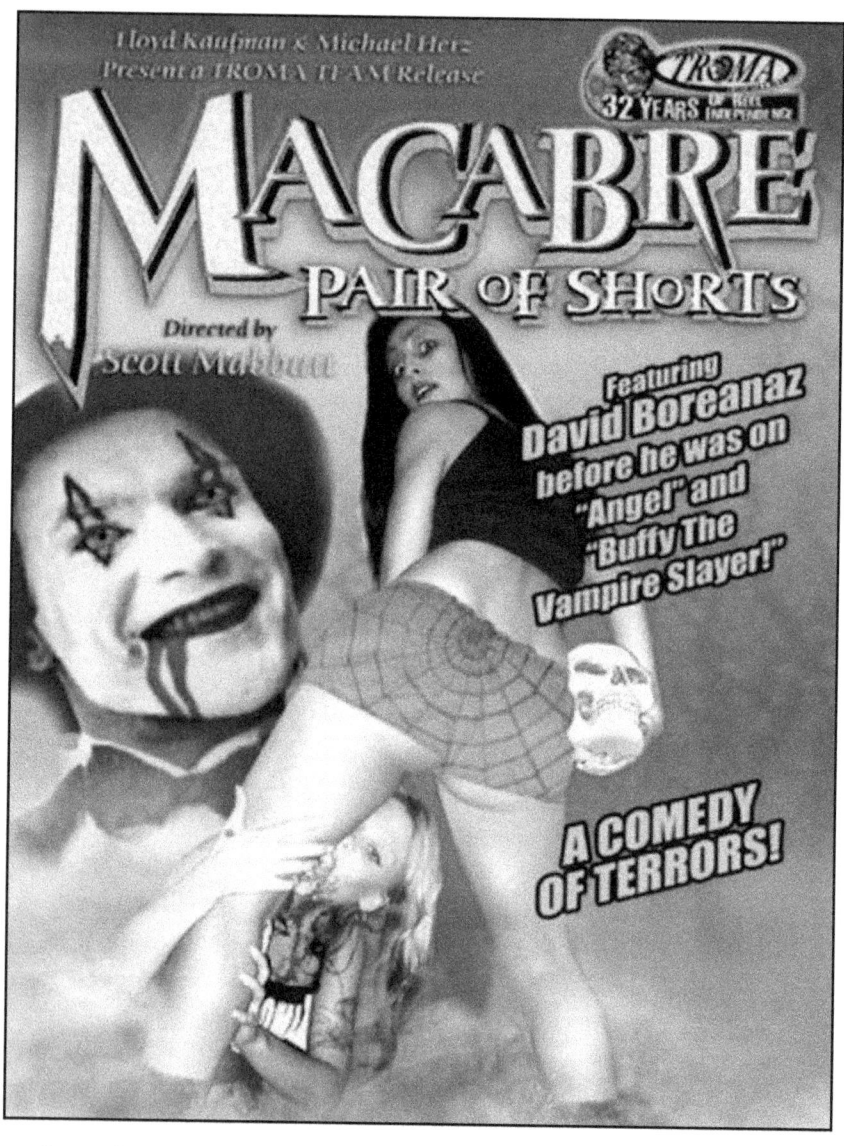

Poster for *Macabre Pair of Shorts*. Photo courtesy of Troma Entertainment.

Michael Overton plays Seymour Hackell, a stuffy and pretentious literature professor obsessed with the Sleep Hollow story. Going as Ichabod Crane to a Halloween party, Hackell is instantly booted for being an obnoxious prick, and with only his bicycle, he enters the "Old Hollow Woods" (of Los Angeles?) on his way home, discovering the real Headless Horseman. Except this is Troma, and the Horsemen isn't actually a Horsemen, but a

Dirt Bike Man. And the headless effect is accomplished by simply pulling the shirt over the actor's head—you know, exactly how you used to do it when you were a headless kid.

Following "The Legend of Seymour Hackell" is "The Eggs," which is almost brilliant. A *Twilight Zone* riff shot in black and white, it concerns a therapist's patient who swears he's being stalked by a Dr. Seuss-like clown, who forces him to eat green eggs and ham. Unfortunately, the filmmakers cannot stick the landing and a good idea ultimately remains just that.

But again, the film picks up steam quickly thereafter as *Macabre Pair of Shorts* (the one that the characters are watching) ends. Cleaning up to go home, our lovable goofs realize the film's celluloid has come to life and is killing everyone in the office. So you know what that means? Yes, a full 20-minute long *Die Hard* parody. I promise you've never seen anything like it.

Hit and miss, but very inspired, *Macabre Pair of Shorts* is worth checking out, if only for "The Legend of Seymour Hackell" and the ending *Die Hard* sequence (called "Overtime").

Kwaidan

| 1965 | Japan | Dir. Masaki Kobayashi |

Look at us gettin' all fancy with the Criterion, art-house shit. One more of these, and I'm gonna start feeling overdressed in this tuxedo.

Masaki Kobayashi's *Kwaidan* is a masterpiece of cinema, a work of such towering magnitude, one cannot help but use the most reductive vocabulary when describing it: beautiful, epic, haunting. Its abstract art design and bright, confident cinematography turn esoteric, Japanese folklore into a cerebral exercise you experience with your gut. (In art appreciation classes, they call this sensation Gut-Brain.)

But for our purposes here, *Kwaidan* is also a horror anthology—though the film hilariously cheats by not utilizing any wraparound framing. Also, with a running time over three hours, every story has enough room to completely flesh itself out, as opposed to a conventional anthology segment that's constrained within a 15–25-minute slot. One story, "Hoichi the Earless" runs for damn near an hour!

The title *Kwaidan* comes from the Japanese word, "kaidan" or ghost story. And while Kobayashi's film delivers a few genuinely chilling sequences, he relies more on mood and atmosphere to conjure a dark Romance. In "The Black Hair," a young samurai ditches his doting wife for greener pastures, only to spend decades pining for her and learning hard the lesson of never taking for granted what's right in front of you. If you've seen the "Lover's Vow" segment from *Tales from the Darkside: The Movie* (1990), "The Woman of the Snow" is a retelling of the same story; a dying woodcutter is spared his life by a *yuki-onna*, a ruthless forest spirit who makes the man promise to never reveal that he saw her. Let's see how that turns out!

The previously mentioned "Hoichi the Earless" concerns a blind musician who gets in over his head performing for ghosts, and "In a Cup of Tea" sees a samurai commit to a futile battle against a whole host of immortal spirits. Like most folkloric parables, none of the stories are particularly complex and meander gracefully along with a minimal soundtrack composed of percussion and small string instruments. Therefore, *Kwaidan* is a film meant to slowly wash over you and intoxicate with its magic. A sit-down-and-get-the-fuck-off-your-phone kind of movie.

Night Train to Terror

| 1985 | United States | Dir. Jay Schlossberg-Cohen |

Making an anthology, you could go the smart route like the *From a Whisper to a Scream* guys and shoot each segment separately. This way, if the project implodes, there is theoretically enough material to piece together a short film or two. Or you can take the *Night Train to Terror* tack and assemble three unfinished horror films into a makeshift anthology with an unrelated, shoehorned wraparound.

Whichever works—or doesn't, in this case. Clever, clunky, and wildly bonkers, the failed experiment of *Night Train to Terror* is an exhilarating experience. Scenes transition nonsensically. Actors mysteriously change hair lengths. Claymation monsters on the level of *Winterbeast* (1992) wreak havoc on clay-ified characters. A new wave band sings and dances in a train car, playing the same song over and over for an hour and a half.

There's oh-so-much to absorb. Not least of all, the wraparound itself, directed by Jay Schlossberg-Cohen, who was tasked by his business partners to anthologize three unfinished films they had produced but couldn't complete. The conceit—which is fairly savvy, given the circumstances—concerns God and Satan conversing on a train that is set to derail in the next hour or two, killing The One Hit Blunders in the car adjacent. To pass the time, the deities peer into the lives of three individuals and argue over the fate of their souls. Each person's story becomes the three segments of the anthology.

The first and least interesting of the trio is "The Case of Harry Billings." The titular character, a strikingly handsome man, is kidnapped by a doctor at an insane asylum and put under hypnosis to lure attractive women back to the institution, where they are murdered for organ harvesting. Unfortunately, the story doesn't lift off in any significant way, despite the fact that the piece is the best edited of the three. I imagine it's tough condensing most of a feature film into a short segment, and it's done efficiently here. The issue is with the material. Though sufficiently sleazy, the entire affair is rather dull in its shortened form, so I can't even picture the experience of watching the film at feature length.

"The Case of Harry Billings" only serves to lower your defenses for what comes next, an immunosuppressant deployed to battle the mild to severe plaque psoriasis that will grow on your brain as a result of finishing the film. And if the inside of your head begins feeling itchy and scaley, that means you've made it to the second story, "The Case of Greta Connors."

Where to start? Well, first of all, the plot is incomprehensible. Built around two subplots from the unfinished film, *Death Wish Club* (1983), the narrative jumps between the love triangle compromised of a wealthy sleazebag, his young lover, and her medical student boyfriend and the death cult they all seemingly belong to. But yeah, yeah, whatever. You come to this story for the outrageous set pieces that the death cult constructs to confront their mortality.

In one particularly memorable (and mind-melting) scene, the cult sits around a kitchen table as a member releases a "Tanzanian Winged Beetle" into the room. The bug, a hideously constructed and bulky prop with glowing eyes, flies around to each character, threatening to land its fatal sting. Instead, the thing just flies out the window, finds two lovers in the park, and plunges a giant stinger into the dude's face, which quickly explodes into a red, pulpy mess.

That's good stuff. Following a couple additional, increasingly elaborate set pieces, you'll find your way to "The Case of Greta Connors," the final and best segment. In fact, it's the only one of the three incomplete films I want to see in its entirety, as the concept is gigantic, involving Nazi demons, holocaust survivors, hardboiled cops, claymation monsters, and an epic showdown between good and evil. It's gobsmacking how Schlossberg-Cohen manages to reduce such a massive scale into a semi-comprehensible short film.

But then again, that's the magic of *Night Train to Terror*. The film shouldn't work, doesn't work, and will never work—even if you recut it a hundred times. Yet, it's impossible to turn away. And not in that rubbernecking, I-want-to-relish-an-absolute-train-wreck kind of way. The movie simply dances to its own rhythm and operates outside any known cinematic language. You've never seen anything like it before or will again. Also, there's a train wreck in which to relish.

Dr. Terror's House of Horrors

| 1965 | United Kingdom | Dir. Freddie Francis |

The one that started it all. Amicus Productions' first horror anthology in a series that birthed the classics, *Tales from the Crypt* (1972), *Asylum* (1972), and the *Vault of Horror* (1973). I wasn't originally planning to include an Amicus film (as they're relatively well-known and revered in the horror community), but I just feel like no one ever talks about *Dr. Terror's House of Horrors*.

And why the hell not? We're talking about Christopher Lee, Peter Cushing, and a baby-faced Donald Sutherland. Werewolves, killer vines, voodoo curses, vampires, and possessed, severed hands, *Evil Dead II*-style. A beautiful, Hammer-esque visual design and classic anthology setup: Cushing plays Doctor Schreck, a practitioner of the metaphysical arts, who predicts the (unfortunate) destinies of his four cabin passengers on a train. (And, honestly, if some guy on the train is telling me in the near future that my family will be terrorized by a sentient weed—I'd believe it!)

Poison

| 1991 | United States | Todd Haynes |

While not a complete, out-and-out horror anthology, Todd Haynes' *Poison* is certainly *out*. An early entry in the New Queer Cinema movement and inspired by the works of French novelist Jean Genet, the film interweaves three stories that share the author's preoccupation with homosexuality, criminality, and otherness. The three pieces—"Hero," "Homo," and "Horror"—play concurrently, each radically different in terms of style and format and heightened by bold drama and surrealist camp.

"Hero" tells its story in the form of a fake, trashy news documentary that is investigating the case of Richie Beacon, a child who allegedly kills his abusive father and flies out the window into the darkness, never to be seen again. "Homo" feels the most like a Genet narrative, concerning a lifelong criminal who becomes sexually infatuated with another man in prison. The most distinct of the three segments, "Horror" is shot in black and white and mimics a classic monster film. In it, a doctor accidentally drinks his scientific creation, a serum made of pure sex drive, and becomes a hideous freak with an insatiable sex drive and a contagious, unsightly skin disease.

Obviously a traditional Mr. Hyde or werewolf application of metaphor, "Horror" is a comment on repressed sexuality. However, in the wake of the AIDS crisis and the subsequent stigmatization of the gay community, the tale takes on another layer and connects directly to the film's first title card, which says "The whole world is dying of panicky fright." The same phrase could easily apply to the sleazy journalism of "Hero" as it dryly mocks the abhorrent sensationalism of an abused and bullied outsider.

Poison is transgressive in the best possible ways, a rebellious "fuck you" to the prude and religious types, and an impassioned and well-crafted defense of a counterculture lifestyle. Highly recommended.

Index

Numbers in **bold** indicate photographs

13 Hours: The Secret Soldiers of Benghazi 6
2001: A Space Odyssey 51

Abar, the First Black Superman 68-69
Abby 68, 76
ABCs of Death, The 161
Adam and Six Eves 27-28
Adamson, Al 76, 77
Alabama's Ghost 73-74
Alien 143, 148
Aliens 65, 66
Alioto, Dean 53, 55
Alligator 19
Almada, Mario 13
Alston, Emmett 159
American Ninja 87, 88
American Pie 45
American Werewolf in London 57
Amsterdamned 19
Anchors, Kelly 150
Anderson, Paul Thomas 135
Ang Kamay ng Diyos 136
Argento, Dario 109, 110
Argenziano, Carmen 72
Arkoff, Sam 15
Ashley, John 138-139, 140, 141, 142
Asylum 161, 170
Atadeniz, Yilmaz 100, 101, 102
Atasoy, Irfan 102
Attack of the 60 Foot Centerfold 40

Attack of the Beast Creatures 134
Attack of the Mushroom People see *Matango*
Avenging Force 87-88

Babatundé, Obba 165
Bad Channels 56
Bad Girls Go to Hell 33-36, **35**
Bad Moon 130
Baker, Carroll 12
Band, Charles 56
Barry, George 127-128, 129
Bashira 121
Bat Pussy 42-43, **43**
Bava, Mario 105, 161
Bay of Blood, A 105
Beaks: The Movie 9
Beast in Space, The 46-47
Beast of Blood 140
Beast of the Yellow Night 140-141
Beast, The 46
Beatty, Ned 97, 98
Behets, Briony 8
Being, The 142-143
Bennett, Marjorie 92
Benton, Helen 120
Berling, Peter 27
Bermuda Triangle, The 12, 22
Bessenger, Mark 149, 150
Big Bird Cage, The 135
Big Doll House, The 135

173

Big Trouble in Little China 77, 150
Bigfoot (1970) 151, 158-159
Bigfoot Wars 158
Bigfoot's Bride 155-156, **156**
Bits and Pieces 111-112
Black Belt Jones 76
Black Christmas 39, 105, 108
Black Devil Doll from Hell 2, 74-76, **75**
Black Emanuelle 68
Black Gestapo, The 77-78
"Black Hair, The" 168
Black Mama, White Mama 68, 141
Black Panther 78
Black Sabbath 161
Black Zoo 4-6, **5**
Black, Cheryl 113
Blade: Trinity 114
Blair Witch Project, The 8, 55, 109
Blind Faith 56
Blob, The (1958) 143
Blood Beat 38, 120
Blood Freak 131-134
Bloodbath in Psycho Town 129
Bloodsuckers from Outer Space 57-58
Blue Fire Lady 49
Bluthal, John 44
Bó, Armando 28, 29
Body Bags 161
Body of a Female 152
Body, The 68
Bolling, Tiffany 39
Bologna, Ugo 20
Boone, David 145, 146
Borowczyk, Walerian 46
Bosque de Muerte 107-108
Boss, Il 99
Bostwick, Barry 130
Bottoms, Timothy 6
Bradley, Al *see* Brescia, Alfonso
Bravo, Ramón 11, 12, 21
Breeders 52-53
Brescia, Alfonso 46
Bride of Frankenstein 155
Brides of Blood 138, **139**
Brock, Alan 153
Bronson, Charles 100

Brooks, Christopher 73
Brooks, Ron 163
Brotherhood of the Wolf 164
Brown, Lester 32
Brown, Timothy 76, 77
Browning, Ricou 85
Bruce, Richard *see* Franklin, Richard
Buechler, John Carl 159, 164
Bullets Bombs and Babes: The Films of Andy Sidaris 90, 93-94, 102-103
"Burning Rubber Tires" 59
Burning, The 113
Burr, Jeff 162
Burrill, Robert L. 126

Caesar, Harry 162
Candy Tangerine Man, The 68
Cannibal Holocaust 99, 115, 155
Cardona III, René 21-23
Cardona Jr., René 9-13, 21, 22
Cardona, René 9, 22
Carlton, Hope Marie 94, 95
Carnada 22
Carne 29
Carpenter, John 51, 77, 150
Carradine, John 158, 159
Carrie (1976) 38
Carter, Jake 70
"Case of Greta Connors, The" 169-170
"Case of Harry Billings, The" 169
Casey, Bernie 7
Castellari, Enzo G. 16, 17, 18
Casus Kiran 100-102
Cat, The 60-61
Catalanato, Joe 154
Cavalcanti, Francisco 110, 111
Celi, Adolfo 99
Cellar Dweller 159
Centerfold Girls, The 39
Centipede Horror 4, 13-14, **14**
Cercle Rouge, Le 98
Chan, Jackie 60
CHiPs 95
Chrome and Hot Leather 77
Chronicles of Riddick, The 114

Chu, Kevin 82
Clark, Bob 39, 97
Clerks 165
Cléry, Corinne 30
Close Encounters of the Third Kind 51
Coburn, Glen 57
Coffy 68, 98
Cohen, Herman 6
"Cold, The" 164
Coleman, Signy 165
Coltrane, Rexx *see* Kong, Jackie
Combs, Jeffrey 164
Come With Me, My Love 37
Contact 101
"Cool Air" 164
Corman, Roger 44, 47, 73, 92, 134, 135, 138, 140, 141, 161
Correll, Michael 150
Cotten, Joseph 10
Cowden, Jack 85
"Crate, The" 125
Creature from Black Lake 154
Creature from the Black Lagoon 85
Creepshow 125, 161
Cronenberg, David 97
Cruel Jaws 16-17, **17**
Cunningham, Sean S. 105, 106
Cushing, Peter 170
Cutt, Michael 157
Cyclone 12-13, 22

Dallas Connection, The 96
Dane, Lawrence 97
Daneliya, Georgiy 61-62
Dangerous Men 88-90
Danning, Sybil 27
Dante, Joe 165
Dark Age 47
Darlene, Gigi 34, **35**
De Gaetano, Alessandro 129
De Leon, Gerardo 136, 138, 140
De Palma, Brian 38
De Roche, Everett 8, 49
Dead of Night 161
Deadly Prey 40
Deadly Weapons 36-37, **36**

Death Bed: The Bed That Eats 127-129, **128**
Death Force 72-73
Death Wish 98, 99, 100
Death Wish 4 87
Death Wish Club 169
Deep Blood 16
Deep Throat 37
Demons 2 65
Demonwarp 159-160
Dennehy, Brian 7
Deodato, Ruggero 98, 99, 114, 156
Derr, Richard 136
Descartes, René 72
Devil's Honey, The 30-31
Di Leo, Antonio 20, 21
Di Leo, Fernando 99
Diamond, Harold 95
Diaz, Vic 140
Dick, Philip K. 84
Die Hard 167
Dildo Heaven 38
Dirty Dozen, The 82, 83
Dirty Harry 98, 99, 100
Disco Godfather 78-80, **79**
Disconnected 38
DMT 56
Do or Die 95-97, **96**
Dohler, Don 63
Dolemite 68
Don't Panic 108
Double Agent 73 37
Dr. Terror's House of Horrors 170
Dreyfuss, Richard 17
"Drowned, The" 164
Drudi, Rossella 65
Dudikoff, Michael 87, 88
Dunn, Terry 150
Dynamite Brothers 76-77

E.T. 52, 59
Each Time I Kill 38
Easter Bunny, Kill! Kill! 106-107
Eat and Run 66
Ebong, Nne 121
Eggleston, Colin 8-9, 45

"Eggs, The" 167
Elliot, Michael 119
Ellis, Dan 114
Enemy Gold 96
Eraserhead 146
Escape from Absolom 82
Espejo, Alejandra 107
Estrada, Erik 95-96
Evil Dead 58, 162
Evil Dead II 57, 148, 170
Exciting Love Girls 46
Expendables, The 82
Extra Terrestrial Visitors 58-60

Face/Off 81
Faces of Death 20
Fanaka, Jamaa 70, 71
Fantasm 44-45, 45, 47, 48-49
Fantasm Comes Again 45
Farley, Teresa 53
Fasano, John 147
Fatal Games 119
Ferda, Sevda 102
Ferrin, Chad 106
Fincher, David 117
Findlay, Michael 34, 111, 152
Findlay, Roberta 152
Firstenberg, Sam 87, 88
Fit to Kill 95
Fitzgibbons, James 120
Flesh Gordon 142
Flipper 85
Food of the Gods, The 14-15
For a Few Dollars More 83
"Four Soldiers" 163
Fragasso, Claudio 65
Francis, Freddie 170
Franciscus, James 17
Frankenheimer, John 91
Franklin, Richard 44, 45, 48
French Connection, The 98
Friday the 13th 105-106, 154
Friday the 13th Part VII 159
Friedman, David F. 25, 26, 27
Friedman, Mike 103
Frizzi, Fabio 156

From a Whisper to a Scream 162-163, 168
From Beyond 159, 163
Frost, Lee 77, 78
Frost, Mark 19
Fuego 28-30
Fulci, Lucio 11, 30, 31, 59, 109, 110

Galindo Jr., Rubén 108
Gamble, Alastair 115
Gamera: Guardian of the Universe 164
Gans, Christophe 163, 164
García Jr., Andrés 11, 12, 13, 107
García, Andrés 107
Garner, James 91
General, The 81
Genet, Jean 170, 171
George, Christopher 7, 112
George, Lynda Day 7, 112
George, Susan 11, 12
Geretta, Geretta 65
Ginnane, Antony I. 44, 47-49
Ginty, Robert 86
Girdler, William 68, 76
Godfather, The 98
Godzilla 16, 125, 126
Golden Queen's Commando 82-83
Goldman, William 82
Good, the Bad, and the Ugly, The 83
Goodbye Uncle Tom 20
Goodman, Diana 87
Gordon, Bert I. 14
Gordon, Robert 4
Gortner, Marjoe 14
Gough, Michael 4, 6
Grand Prix 91
Grave Robbers 108
Green Slime, The 86
Grier, Pam 89, 135, 141
Grinter, Brad 131, 133
Grizzly 4, 17
Gulager, Clu 162
Guns 95
Gutterballs 114-115
Guyana: Crime of the Century 9

Hahn, Jess 86
Halloween (1978) 37, 105-106
Halloween II 106
Halsey, Brett 30
Hanson, Tom 117, 118
Hard Boiled 60
Hard Hunted 95
Hard Target 88
Hard Ticket to Hawaii 94-95, **94**, 102, 103-104
Hargreaves, John 8
Harmstorf, Raimund 27
Harryhausen, Ray 15
Hart, Christopher 66
Hawkes, Steve 133
Haynes, Todd 170
Heitmann, Carlheinz 27
Henriksen, Lance 60
Henry: Portrait of a Serial Killer 111
"Hero" 171
Hidden, The 61
Hill, Jack 68, 135, 141
Hill, John Beaton 149
Hill, Walter 88
Hinton, Darby 93
Hinzman, S. William 115, 116
Hipp, Paul 56
Hobbs, Frederic 68, 73, 74
Hodder, Kane 130
"Hoichi the Earless" 167, 168
Hollywood Chainsaw Hookers 40
Holmes, John C. **45**, 45
"Homo" 171
Honda, Ishirō 15-16
Honeymoon Horror 112-113
Hong, James 77
Hora do Medo, A 110-111
"Horror" 171
Horrors of the Black Museum 6
House by the Cemetery, The 59
House on Sorority Row, The 108
House on the Edge of the Park, The 115
Hoven, Adrian 26, 27
Huston, John 9, 60

I Know What You Did Last Summer 108, 122
I Still Know What You Did Last Summer 105
Iglehart, James 72
Immoral Mr. Teas, The 28
"In a Cup of Tea" 168
In the Shadow of Kilimanjaro 6-7
Inglorious Bastards, The 17, 82
Inner Sanctum 40
Invasion of the Aluminum People 145-147, **146**
Invasion of the Body Snatchers (1956) 51, 146
Invasion of the Body Snatchers (1978) 51
Invasion U.S.A. 87
Irving, Washington 161, 165
Island of Doctor Moreau, The 141
Island of Lost Souls 141
It Happened at Lakewood Manor 7-8

Jacopetti, Gualtiero 20
Jaeckel, Richard 85, 86
James, Steve 87
Jason and the Argonauts 125
Jaws 4, 11, 16, 17, 18, 63, 143
Jesus Shows You the Way to the Highway 83-84, **84**
Jones, Shirley L. 74, **75**
Jonze, Spike 156
Jordan, Michael B. 78

Kai, Lam Ngai 60, 61
Kaneko, Shusuke 163, 164
Keach, Sr., Stacy 7
Keaton, Buster 81
Kelly, Jim 76
Kennedy, Arthur 12
Kennedy, George 159, 160
Kennedy, Jayne 72
Kennedy, Leon Isaac 72
Kennedy, Shannon 159, 160
Kersey, Paul 100
Keyholes Are for Peeping 36
Kid, William 123-124

Kilink Istanbul'da 101
Kill List 153
Killerspiele see *Fatal Games*
Killing Touch, The see *Fatal Games*
Kincaid, Tim 52, 53
Kin-dza-dza! 61-63
King Kong 158
King Kong vs. Godzilla 16
Kiser, Terry 162
Kobayashi, Masaki 167-168
Kolobos 108-110, **109**, 121-124
Kong, Jackie 142-143
Konga 6
Kruse, Majken 92
Kwaidan 167-168

L.E.T.H.A.L. Ladies: Return to Savage Beach 93, 96
"L'Estasi Dell'oro" 83
Landau, Martin 143
Lane, Sirpa 46, 47
Lanier, Didi 163
Lansing, Joi 158
Last House on the Left, The 112
Last Shark, The 16-18, **17**
Leatherface: The Texas Chainsaw Massacre III 162
Lederer, Francis 136, 137
Lee, Christopher 170
Lee, Waise 61
"Legend of Seymour Hackell, The" 165-167
"Legend of Sleepy Hollow, The" 165
Leroget, Ferenc 143, 144
Let's Scare Jessica to Death 153
Lethal Weapon 63
Lewald, Candace 115
Lewis, Hershell Gordon 34, 133
Lewman, Lance 52
Li, Keith 13
Li, Margaret **14**, 14
Liatowitsch, Daniel 108, 109, 110, 121
"Library, The" 164
License to Kill 11
Lin, Brigitte 83
Live and Let Die 68, 112

Live Like a Cop, Die Like a Man 98-100
Llansó, Miguel 83, 84
Long Swift Sword of Siegfried, The 26-27
Long Weekend 8-9, 45, 49
Looman, Julian 19
Lorna 33
Love Toy 36
Lovecraft, H.P. 61, 161, 163-164
"Lovecraft's Traveling Amusements" 163
Lovelock, Ray 99
"Lover's Vow" 168
Low Life 89
Lucas, George 100
Lussier, Sheila 112
Lynn, Kane W. 135, 136, 138, 140

Maas, Dick 18, 19
Mabbutt, Scott 165
Macabre Pair of Shorts 165-167, **166**
Macaulay, Charles 142
Mad Doctor of Blood Island 138-140
Mad Max 44, 49
Madia, Stefano 30
"Maggie" 99
Magnificent Seven, The 83
Majorettes, The 115-116
Malibu Express 93-94
Mandy 59
Maniac 111
Mann, Michael 98
Marie, Charlotte 106
Marins, José Mojica 111
Marsillach, Blanca 30
Martinelli, Marcello 41
Marvin, Little 68
Marzilli, John 129
Matango 15-16
Mateo, Augustin 83
Matinee 165
Mattei, Bruno 2, 16, 64, 65
Mayne, Belinda 86, 87
Mayo, Tobar 69
McPherson Tape, The 53-55, **54**
Melville, Jean-Pierre 98
Merlin, Jan 142
Meyer, Bess 164

Meyer, Russ 25, 28, 33, 34
Meyers, Thom 57
Milian, Tomas 99
Miller, George 48
Milpitas Monster, The 126-127
Mitchum, Christopher 158
Mitchum, John 158
Miu, Michael 13
Mondo Cane 20
Monster of Camp Sunshine, The 143-145, **144**
Monte, Marlo 70, **70**, 71
Moore, Geoffrey 95
Moore, Rudy Ray 78-80, **79**
Morgan, Chesty 36-37, **36**
Morita, Pat 95
Morricone, Ennio 83
Morrow, Vic 18
Moss, Ron **94**, 95
Most Dangerous Game, The 88
Motorpsycho 34
"MPS" 165
Mr. No Legs 85-86
Muskatell, Timothy 106
Muthers, The 68, 73
My Brilliant Career 44
Mysterious Island 134
Mystery Science Theater 3000 2, 58

Necronomicon 62, 163-165
Nero, Franco 60, 99
Nicholson, Ryan 114
Nicolaou, Ted 56
Night Court 78
Night of a Thousand Cats 4, 10-11, 23
Night of the Bloody Apes 9
Night of the Demon (1980) 155, 157-158
Night of the Living Dead (1968) 116
Night to Dismember, A 37-38
Night Train to Terror 38, 168-170
Nightbeast 63-64, **64**
Ninja Zombie 149-150, **149**
Norris, Chuck 87
Nude on the Moon 32-33, **33**

O'Neill, David Michael 160
Obregon, Rodrigo 104
Ocvirk, Todd 108, 109, 110, 121-124
Olympic Nightmare see *Fatal Games*
"On the Run" 162-163
Orcutt, Bill 31
Ortigoza, Carlos David 107, 108
Osco, William 142-143
Oswalt, Patton 127, 128
Outer Limits, The 114
"Overtime" 167
Overton, Michael 166

Packard, Frank 68
Palance, Jack 86, 159
Pallardy, Jean-Marie 86
Papaya, Love Goddess of the Cannibals 46
Paradisi, Giulio 60
Patel, Raju 6, 7
Patrick 44, 47, 49
Paul, Don Michael 97
Paulsen, Pat 58
Payne, Bruce 164
Peckinpah, Sam 60
Penitentiary 70
Perry, Rod 77, 78
Pettyjohn, Angelique 139
Peyser, John 39
Peyton, Claudia 120
Phantom Planet, The 51
Phantom, The 150
Phifer, Mekhi 105
Picasso Trigger 95
Picnic at Hanging Rock 44, 48
Pieces 58, 59, 112
Pierce, Jack 125, 136
Piranha 17
Plan 9 from Outer Space 1
Pod People see *Extra Terrestrial Visitors*
Poison 170-171
Police Academy 112
Porel, Marc 99
Porky's 45
Possessed by the Night 39-41
Predator 65, 159

Preston, Harry 112
Price, Vincent 162
Prine, Andrew 39
Prior, Ted 40
Project Metalbeast 129-130
Prosperi, Franco E. 20
Pryor, Richard 83
Psycho 105, 106, 111
Psycho II 44
Pumpkinhead II 162

Quinn, Martha 56

Racing Scene, The 91
Rad, John S. *see* Yeganehrad, Jahangir Salehi
Raiders of the Lost Ark 100
Raimi, Sam 162
Randall, Anne 92
"Rats in the Wall, The" 164
Ray, Fred Olen 39, 40
Re-Animator 56, 163, 164
Real World, The 109, 123
Redford, Robert 83
Reemes, Harry 37
Reeves, Steve 147
Reitman, Ivan 97
Remy, Ronald 140
Repulsion 123
Return of the Living Dead 57, 58
Revenge of the Ninja 88
Reyonoso, Jorge 107
Rhys-Davies, John 6
Rivera, Jessica Megan 155
Roadgames 44, 45
Robinson Crusoe on Mars 51
Robinson, Charles P. 77, 78
Robot Chicken 84
Robowar 65
Rock 'n' Roll Nightmare 63, 147-148
Rolling Thunder 98
Rolling Vengeance 97-98
Rombin, Hillevi 29
Romero, Eddie 68, 73, 134, 135-142
Romero, George 57, 116
Rumble in the Bronx 60

Russo, John 116
Ryan, John P. 77, 87-88

S.W.A.T. 77
Salvatori, Renato 99
Samouraï, Le 98
Santiago, Cirio H. 68, 72-73
Sarli, Isabel 28, 29
Satan Was a Lady 37
Savage Beach 95
Savini, Tom 164
Saw 110, 121, 122
Sayles, John 19
Scalps 40
Scheerer, Robert 7
Schlossberg-Cohen, Jay 168, 170
Scott, Ridley 143
Scream 108, 109, 122
Scum of the Earth! 34
Seven 92-93
Seventh Curse, The 61
Sexy Proibitissimo 41-42
Shackleton, Allan 152
Shaft 67
Shaw Brothers 60, 84
Shaw, Robert 18
Sherman, Samuel M. 138
Shining, The 124
Shocking Dark 2, 64-66
Shogun Assassin 17
Shriek of the Mutilated 152-153
Sidaris, Andy 90-97, 102-104
Sidaris, Arlene 93-94, 102-104
Sidaris, Christian 96
Silva, Henry 19, 40, 41
Silver, Ron 66
Simón, Juan Piquer 58, 59
Sinclair, Joshua 18
Sinfoney, Sykotic 56
Sivero, Frank 41
Slatzer, Robert F. 158
Slaughter, The 152
Slinker, Ron 85, 86
Slugs 58, 59
Smith, Suzanna 112
Smith, William 92

Smokey and the Bandit 112
Snapshot 44, 49
Solaris 16
Somers, Suzanne 7
Soul Vengeance see *Welcome Home Brother Charles*
Southbound 161
Southern Comfort 88
Spafford, Susan 59
Speed, Carol 76-77
Spielberg, Steven 17, 18, 59, 142, 143
Spier, Dona 94, 95, **96**
Spy Smasher 101, 102
Stacey 91-92, 93
Stander, Lionel 12
"Stanley" 162
Stanley, Michael 134
Star Trek 46, 51
Starman 51
Starsky & Hutch 99
Stepfather II 162
Stern, Steven Hilliard 97
Stetler, Lyle 59
Stiglitz, Hugo 9, 10, 11, 12, 13, 23
Story of Ricky, The 60
Strain, Julie 104
Strange Days 40
Supercop 60
Superfly 67
Superman IV 69
Survive! 9, 12, 13, 22
Suspiria 110, 123, 124
Sutherland, Donald 170
Sweet Sweetback's Baadasssss Song 67, 148
Sword of Vengeance 17
Sympathy in Summer 49

Tadesse, Daniel 83
Tales from the Crypt 16, 112, 161, 170
Tales from the Darkside: The Movie 168
Tales from the Hood 161
Tales from the QuadeaD Zone 75
Tales of Terror 161
Tang, Alan 76
Tarantino, Quentin 72, 135, 142

Taylor, Ed 121
Teenagers from Outer Space 51
Terminator 38, 60, 61, 65, 66
Terminator 2 13, 81
Terror in the Swamp 154
Terror Is a Man 136-138, **137**, 140
TerrorVision 56
Tetsuo: The Iron Man 146
Them 68-69
There Will Be Blood 6
Thing from Another World, The 143
Thing, The (1982) 51, 159
Thirst 44
Thomas, Leland 111, 112
Thor, Jon Mikl 63, 147, 148
Three Stigmata of Palmer Eldritch, The 84
Thunder Among the Leaves 28
Thyssen, Greta 136
Tintorera 11-12, 21-22
Toshimitsu, Teizō 126
Touch of Her Flesh, The 34, 152
Trancers 56
Travolta, John 81
Trick 'r Treat 161
Trilogy of Terror 134
Troll 159
Troll 2 65
Turkey Shoot 44, 47
Turner, Chester N. 68, 74, 75
Tweed, Shannon 40, 41
Twilight People 141-142
Twilight Zone: The Movie 161
Tyler, Haven 65

Uncaged 18-19
Unheimliche Geschichten 161
Urban Legend 108, 122

Valdez, Ronaldo 139
Valentine 108
Van Cleef, Lee 99
Van Damme, Jean-Claude 81, 88
Van Peebles, Melvin 67
Van Winden, Sophie 19
Vasquez, Roberta 95, **96**

Vault of Horror 170
Vengeance Is Mine see *Death Force*
Visitor, The 60
Vollrath, Ted 81, 85-86

Wagner, Bob 113
Wagoner, J. Robert 78
Waithe, Lena 68
Wake in Fright 8, 44
Wallis, John 27
War of the Worlds (1953) 51
Warner, David 164
Wasson, James C. 157
Watanabe, Akira 126
Weaver, Michael 150
Weber, Amy 109
Welcome Home Brother Charles 70-71, **70**
Wells, H.G. 15, 51, 141
West, Adam 83
What Do You Say to a Naked Waiter? 147
When I Die I'll Make Films in Hell: Doris Wishman in Miami 31
Whisperer in Darkness, The 164
"Whispers" 164, 165
White Fire 86-87
Whitman, Stuart 9
Wide World of Sports 91
Wiesmeier, Lynda 93
Wilcox, Mary 140
Wilczkowska, Joseph 36
Wilczkowska, Liliana see Morgan, Chesty
Wild Beasts 3, 20-21
Wild Geese, The 82
Williams, Treat 18, 150
Williamson, Fred 86
Winner, Michael 100
Winterbeast 168
Wishman, Doris 25, 31-38
Wofford, Erick 155, 156
"Woman of the Snow, The" 168
"Won't Take Too Long" 99
Woo, John 60

Wood, Ed 53, 133, 146, 160
Woodell, Pat 142
Wray, Fay 158
Wyckoff, Michael 112

X-Files, The 114

Yagi, Kanji 126
Yeganehrad, Jahangir Salehi 88, 89
Yun-fat, Chow 60, 61
Yuzna, Brian 163, 164, 165

Zaphiratos, Fabrice-Ange 120
Zodiac 117
Zodiac Killer, The 117-119, **118**
Zombi 2 11, 110
Zygmont, S.E. 111

www.ingramcontent.com/pod-product-compliance
Lightning Source LLC
Chambersburg PA
CBHW051056160426
43193CB00010B/1207